THE
ENLIGHTENMENT
TRADITION

THE
ENLIGHTENMENT
TRADITION

ROBERT ANCHOR

UNIVERSITY OF CALIFORNIA PRESS

BERKELEY, LOS ANGELES, LONDON

In Memory of Lynne and the joy we shared

CONTENTS

A PARTIAL CHRONOLOGY

1758   Quesnay's *Economic Table.*

1759   Voltaire's *Candide.*

1762   Rousseau's *The Social Contract* and *Emile.*

1762–1796   The reign of Catherine II (the Great) of Russia.

1763   Peace of Paris signed by Britain, France, and Spain. Treaty of Hubertusburg signed by Prussia and Austria.

1767   Lessing's *Hamburg Dramaturgy* and *Minna von Barnhelm.*

1772   First partition of Poland by Prussia, Austria, and Russia. Lessing's *Emilia Galotti.*

1774   Accession of Louis XVI. Fall of Maupeou and recall of the parlements. Treaty of Kutchuk-Kainardji signed by Russia and Turkey. Pugachev's uprising in Russia. Goethe's *Werther.*

1776   American Declaration of Independence. Adam Smith's *The Wealth of Nations.*

1778   Death of Voltaire and Rousseau.

1780–1790   The reign of Joseph II of Austria.

1781   Kant's *Critique of Pure Reason.*

1784   First books of Herder's *Ideas on a Philosophy of History of Mankind* and Schiller's *Love and Intrigue.*

1788   Kant's *Critique of Practical Reason.*

1789   Calling of the Estates General in France and proclamation of the *Declaration of the Rights of Man and of the Citizen.*

EDITOR'S INTRODUCTION

Historians use the term "Enlightenment" as both a noun and an adjective. Used as a noun, the term designates a period of exceptionally consistent cultural creativity that lasted from the English Revolution of 1688 to the French Revolution of 1789. When used as an adjective, however, as in "the Enlightenment tradition," the term denotes a specific attitude of mind that gradually gained ascendancy among European intellectuals during that period.

The Enlightenment attitude of mind was complex and internally varied, but it can be characterized roughly as a dedication to human reason, science, and education as the best means of building a stable society of free men on earth. This meant that the Enlightenment was inherently suspicious of religion, hostile to tradition, and resentful of any authority based on custom or faith alone. Ultimately the Enlightenment was nothing if not secular in its orientation; it offered the first program in the history of mankind for the construction of a human community out of natural materials alone.

During the French Revolution and immediately after it, Enlightenment ideals were subjected to searching criticism as the principal inspiration behind the radicalism of the Jacobins. But by mid-nineteenth century those ideals, appropriately revised, qualified, and reconstituted as "Liberalism," had once more been established as the distinctive world-view of Western man. And Western man entered the twentieth century armed with Enlightenment values to face the challenges of mass society and technological culture on a world scale. Thus, the crisis into which Liberal society entered during the twentieth century was, ultimately, a crisis of the Enlightenment tradition. It is not surprising, therefore, that much of the best contemporary thought takes the form of an attack upon or defense of the original Enlightenment. Today many thinkers believe that there were fundamental flaws in the Enlightenment faith in reason, science, and education. They oppose that faith in the name of irrationality, intuition, and an elitist conception of human nature that reserves education for the genetically gifted alone. Given the central place occupied by the Enlightenment tradition in the current debate over the future of Western civilization, an analysis of that tradition must have not only a historical interest but a pressing current interest as well.

Robert Anchor surveys the Enlightenment in its heroic age—the eighteenth century. His main thesis is that although there were contradictions in Enlightenment culture, these were not so much contradictions *within* its ideals but *between* its ideals and the specific aims of the class that represented them in the social, economic, and political arenas during the late eighteenth and early nineteenth centuries.

Throughout the eighteenth century, Anchor maintains, the bourgeoisie, in France especially but also in the rest of Europe, criticized the aristocratic and despotic Old Regime in the name of values that were later incapsulated in the Revolutionary motto: "Liberty, Equality, and Fraternity." Spokesmen for the bourgeoisie justified their appeal to these values on the authority of two, more abstract and more metaphysical, concepts: Reason, conceived not merely as a tool but as a substantive attribute of humanity and Nature, viewed as an autonomous, harmonious, and self-regulating mechanism of material bodies connected by mathematically definable causal relationships. The Old Regime was dedicated to defending the institution of absolute monarchy and the privileges of a hereditary nobility. It depended upon tradition, custom, and convention for its sanctions. Bourgeois ideologists criticized the Old Regime by holding up an image of a society unencumbered by historical restrictions. Their ideal society would be responsive to the immediate needs and desires of every individual, governed by reason, and would guarantee the life, liberty, and property of all. This image appealed to disaffected elements of literate classes all over Europe: nobility, clergy, and bourgeoisie alike. All the literate classes of Europe promoted the ideals of the Enlightenment during the first half of the eighteenth century, under the misconception that their realization could not fail to benefit them in the way that each desired.

But, Anchor insists, there was a basic ambiguity in the enlighteners' demand for a freer society. In part this was the fault of the *philosophes*, both aristocratic and bourgeois, who obscured the differences between the *rights* they demanded for all men and the *privileges* that they thought it possible to grant them as individuals. Although they spoke of "Liberty, Equality, and Fraternity" in terms that appealed to everyone suffering from the inequities of the Old Regime, their conceptions of how those values were to be implemented remained locked within narrowly restricted class aspirations and goals. When an aristocrat attacked the monarchy in the name of freedom, he tacitly assumed that freedom meant a greater opportunity to fulfill himself in peculiarly aristocratic ways, which implied greater restrictions on a restless and aggressive bourgeoisie. Conversely, when a bourgeois intellectual demanded more

freedom for mankind, he tended to identify the freedom of
mankind with the aspirations of the middle class in the
economic and social fields.

But there was a further ambiguity *within* the bourgeois class over the meaning of the terms "Liberty, Equality,
and Fraternity." When middle-class *philosophes* spoke of
the rights of men within a political context, they seemed
to be championing a classical, humanistic conception of the
ideal citizen, who would suppress his private interests
whenever they conflicted with the general welfare of the
group to which he belonged. However, when they spoke
of the rights of men within an economic or social context,
they seemed to assume that humanity was nothing more
than a congeries of isolated individuals, each competing
with every other in an enmity and strife that lasted unto
death.

Anchor holds that these many ambiguities in the
Enlightenment ideology were masked throughout the
greater part of the eighteenth century by a myth that lay
at the very heart of the enlighteners' optimism: the myth
of the "hidden hand." This myth assumed that there was a
basic harmony of interests among men *in the long run,* and
that it was only necessary to release everyone to pursue
freely his own self-interest in order to realize a harmonious
social order, similar to that which reigned in nature, in the
end. The conviction that harmony was the "natural" product
of strife, that unity resulted "naturally" from diversity, un-
derlay the gleefulness with which Enlightenment thinkers
undertook destruction of every idea, institution, and value
inherited from the older, religiously oriented culture of the
Middle Ages. Gradually, however, as the eighteenth century
passed its mid-point, the myth of the "hidden hand" was
brought under severe criticism. By the end of the century

it had dissipated. The result was that the two contradictory conceptions of human nature, which it had formerly unified, were disengaged from one another; the two classes, aristocracy and bourgeoisie, which had originally promoted Enlightenment ideals in tandem, were mutually alienated from one another; Western European society was sundered into mutually antagonistic classes prepared to destroy one another in a war to the death. This set the stage for the class warfare that characterized the French Revolution during its more radical and its more reactionary phases between 1789 and 1815.

Anchor's analysis of the Enlightenment tradition proceeds in the following way. After a preliminary discussion of the current debate over the nature of the Enlightenment in the first part, he turns, in the second part, to the social, political, and economic substructure of Enlightenment culture during the early eighteenth century. He concentrates on France, for France's role was crucial in the development of Enlightenment ideals precisely because it possessed an entrenched aristocracy on the one side and a powerful middle class on the other, with about equal social power by the middle of the century. In Central and Eastern Europe there was no middle class to speak of; in England the middle class had already been assimilated into an essentially aristocratic, but ultimately flexible, social order by the end of the seventeenth century. In France, however, the aristocracy had grown resentful of the restrictions placed upon it by Louis XIV and it was waiting for a chance to regain its lost feudal privileges as soon as the opportunity offered itself. The French bourgeoisie was strong and growing in strength. It resented the privileges that the older aristocracy still possessed, it wanted access to similar privileges, and it had begun to resent the king's policy of keeping the classes functionally divided in order to dominate them individually more easily. The bourgeoisie, therefore, was also ready to reorder society when and if the occasion presented itself. And it was especially receptive to any ideas that might be used to support the notion that such reordering should constitute a new kind of society and not attempt a return to a lost and imperfect, aristocratic past.

Bourgeois ideologists found the desired revolutionary ideas in the work of two Englishmen, Newton and Locke, who were regarded as anything but revolutionary on their home ground. Newton was recognized as the greatest scientific genius of his age; he had established, apparently for all time, the essential order, harmony, and self-regulating quality of the physical world. Locke had seemingly shown how society itself could be transformed into a similarly self-regulating mechanism by criticism, reform, and revision of any tradition that prohibited men from fully exercising the rights provided them at birth by nature. Locke's ideas had been fully worked out as a means of justifying the English Revolution of 1688. In the *post*-revolutionary situation in which they had been expounded, however, they were less a radical call to action than a consoling rationalization of the revolution that had already occurred. But when the ideas of Newton and Locke were introduced into the highly charged atmosphere of France in the 1730s, they were pregnant with revolutionary consequences; for they struck at the very principles upon which monarchical and aristocratic society were constituted. For the next half century the ideas of Newton and Locke were discussed, debated, and carried to their logical conclusions as potential criticisms of any received tradition, in culture and society. The systematic application of Newton's philosophy of nature and Locke's philosophy of society to the traditional culture of Continental Europe was primarily the work of the French *phi-losophes*; they, more than any other, gave the distinctive form to the Enlightenment tradition as we know it.

The third and fourth parts of Anchor's essay consist of a detailed analysis of the internal logic of this applica-tion. In his consideration of the work of Montesquieu, Prévost, and Voltaire, he traces the transition from the *philosophes'* original optimism to their later apprehension that perhaps man's physical nature was not reconcilable with his moral aspirations. He outlines the *philosophes'* dis-cussions of man's obligation to the past as against his re-sponsibility to the present, their debate over the conflict of public duties with private rights. He shows how the aristocratic and conservative Montesquieu took a certain heroic pride in the dual obligations under which man la-bored in his attempts to build a good society on earth; how the gifted Abbé Prévost dramatized the conflict between natural impulses on the one side and moral sensibility on the other in his tender novel, *Manon Lescaut*; how the dynamic Voltaire carried on his fight for human dignity and freedom in the face of a growing conviction that Stoic resignation was perhaps the highest goal to which a serious man might aspire. The essential ambivalence of Enlighten-ment thought was ruthlessly laid bare by the English philosopher David Hume; Anchor shows how Hume antici-pated most of the problems that devotees of the Enlighten-ment tradition would have to face in the future.

Then, in the fourth part, he analyzes the attempt of the great materialists, La Mettrie, Holbach, Helvétius, and Diderot, to build a free society on the basis of a consistently mechanistic conception of the physical world and man, which foredoomed them to a fall into a crippling fatalism. Here a basic flaw of Enlightenment thinking was driven home to consciousness. For if, as the materialists believed on the authortiy of Newton, man was nothing but an aggregation of atomic particles governed by ineluctable laws of cause and effect, then how was it possible to join them together in self-transcending communities of mutual service and love? The materialists could provide no answer to this question, but they did not quit the field without a fight. In Quesnay, the greatest of the Physiocrats, and Diderot, the first modern dialectician, they succeeded in revising the conventional conceptions of society and human nature. Quesnay tried to solve the problem by transposing the inevitable competition between men to the international plane while restricting and directing it in the general interest of the nation internally. Diderot added a new dimension to Enlightenment thinking by his profound psychological inquiries; he concluded that a theory of human nature that encompassed the possible evolution of human consciousness dared conclude that man might be more than *mere* nature in the long run.

It was the passionate and rebellious Rousseau who raised Enlightenment thought to a new level of moral awareness. Anchor sees Rousseau less as the enemy of the Enlightenment than as its consummation. Rousseau still retained the optimism of the early enlighteners, their fighting and critical spirit, their respect for Nature against custom and tradition, and their vision of a free humanity. Contrary to common opinion, Rousseau even retained their respect for Reason. But Rousseau added to all this a profound analysis of the emotions, the senses, and sentiment, making them the center of human suffering and achievement, and also investing them with the power to direct man in his quest for genuine community. Thus, according to Anchor, Rousseau signals the Enlightenment's loss of faith in nature

as an ultimate authority in moral matters. Rousseau honored, even worshipped, the "natural" against the "artificial,"
but he never entertained the hope that man could return
to the primitive state of preconscious existence, nor did he
desire to return to such a state. He pressed his thought on
to the future, to a human world that existed beyond both
nature and society, and approximated true community. In
Rousseau the Enlightenment produced its most subtle utopian. It also produced the founder of a new, peculiarly
modern humanism. Rousseau showed his age that if man
wanted a life better than he had, he could not depend upon
any transhistorical agency to provide it for him; he would
have to create it himself, in pain and suffering, and on
behalf of a morality that honored the inner man as well as the
outer.

The fifth part proceeds to an analysis of two possible
consequences of Rousseau's revelation of nature's inadequacy as a source of moral authority. The infamous Marquis
de Sade showed the absurdity of any attempt to base
morality on nature. Since nature was neutral, any attempt
to live by a naturalistic ethic led to nihilism, so de Sade
taught. The German philosopher Kant, by contrast, tacitly
recognizing this argument, grounded morality precisely in
man's capacity to resist natural impulses. Thus, by the end
of the eighteenth century, Kant had rescued man from the
tyranny of both society and nature, finding his essential
humanity in a concept of consciousness that had been expanded to also include the will in addition to reason.
In Kant, Anchor argues, the most creative strains of the
English, French, and German phases of the Enlightenment were temporarily synthesized: Hume, Rousseau,
and Leibniz all have a place in Kant's system. But the
Kantian synthesis was too subtle, too intricate, to weather

the winds of Revolution that swept over Europe in 1789. Kant's synthesis was no sooner achieved than it began to be broken down once more and reduced to simpler elements. This was the work of the German *Sturm und Drang*, the last phase of the Enlightenment and the launching stage of Romanticism.

During the *Sturm und Drang*, Enlightenment ideas were reexamined, sublimated, and made a basis for an idealistic humanism that would constitute the axis of Western thought during the next historical epoch. Herder, Schiller, and especially Goethe found in the concept of personal culture (*Bildung*) a value, which, in their view, took precedence over the narrow hedonism and utilitarianism of the original Enlightenment. Emphasis now shifted to the individual's struggle with nature and society, not in the interest of "bettering" himself, but in the interest of "realizing" himself in the full exercise of his powers, both physical and spiritual. But this was no narrow individualism, as Goethe defined it; individualism found its limit in the ideal Humanity, which Goethe, like Herder, saw fashioning itself over the whole of historical time.

From the deification of Nature to the deification of Humanity—this was the course that Enlightenment thought followed as it made its way from England through France to Germany during the eighteenth century. In that transition Western thought secured some of its most precious principles. But at the same time, if Anchor is correct, those principles had become disengaged from its original carrying class, the bourgeoisie, and all but antithetical to Society in general. While Enlightenment thought had become progressively more idealistic the middle class itself had become more narrowly materialistic in its aspirations. While Enlightenment intellectuals had progressively become citizens of the world, the bourgeoisie had become increasingly the champions of limited class and national interests. All this prepared Europe for that fatal schism between the intelligentsia and society that characterized the century that followed. The nineteenth century was a century of triumph for the bourgeoisie all over Europe—and the world. But at the time of its greatest triumphs, the middle class found its severest critics in the heirs of the Enlightenment: Marx, Nietzsche, Freud, and their followers. By the beginning of the twentieth century, the Enlightenment in both its intellectual and its social sides had finally reached its culmination; in the division between intellectuals and society that has plagued this century, the Enlightenment has borne its richest, and most bitter, fruit.

HAYDEN V. WHITE

AUTHOR'S NOTE

In all cases where only the author's name appears with a quote in the text—the sole exception being Clough et al., p. 28—the title of the work is given in the bibliography.

THE
ENLIGHTENMENT
TRADITION

THE PROBLEM
OF THE
ENLIGHTENMENT

Liberty, then, about which so many volumes have been written, is when accurately defined, only the power of acting.

—Voltaire

Whoever reasons rightly, invents, and whoever desires to invent must be able to reason. Only those who are not fitted for either believe that they can separate the one from the other.

—Lessing

During the dark depression year of 1931, the noted American historian, Carl Becker, delivered a series of lectures on the Enlightenment which were published under the title, *The Heavenly City of the Eighteenth-Century Philosophers*. This book, which has since become a minor classic, set forth the then novel thesis that the eighteenth century was far closer in its basic values and world-view to the thirteenth century than to the twentieth. "There is more of Christian philosophy in the writings of the *philosophes* than has yet been dreamt of in our histories," wrote

1

Becker. The century of Voltaire, like that of Aquinas, was rational and theological in outlook, Becker argued, whereas ours was concerned mainly with fact and function. The modern world had replaced theology, philosophy, and deductive logic by history, science, and empirical techniques, and viewed things as "changing entities . . . points in an endless process of differentiation, of unfolding, of waste and repair." In contrast to the "climate of opinion—those instinctively held preconceptions in the broad sense"— of the thirteenth and eighteenth centuries, our own age finds man as "but a foundling in the universe, abandoned by the forces that created him. Unparented, unassisted and undirected by omniscient or benevolent authority, he must fend for himself, and with the aid of his own limited intelligence find his way about in an indifferent universe." In our century, in the words of Aristophanes, "Whirl is king, having deposed Zeus."

Becker has been criticized, and rightly so, for having exaggerated both the similarities in outlook between the thirteenth and eighteenth centuries and the discontinuity in outlook between the eighteenth and twentieth. Even if it be granted that the eighteenth century was an "age of faith as well as of reason," and that the thirteenth was an "age of reason as well as of faith," there are still questions: whether faith or reason dominated; how they were interrelated; what the object of each was. While it is true that the basic components of the Enlightenment world-view— the rejection of original sin, the conception of the universe as an infinite, self-contained, rationally ordered phenomenon, and the advocacy of intellectual self-reliance—were rooted in earlier centuries (though not notably in the Middle Ages), it is also true that the *philosophes* used these ideas to topple the feudal, ecclesiastical establishment and medieval religious world-view, not to support them. By freeing science and history from theology and metaphysics, the Enlightenment made a major advance in the direction of our secular, materialistic, "modern" culture.

Moreover, the "climate of opinion" of any age is not something disembodied and self-generating, as Becker seemed to suggest, but rather is enmeshed in the concrete social and historical context in which it comes into being. The modern world-view is closely bound up with a number of significant developments, many of which link the eighteenth with the nineteenth and twentieth centuries. Among them are the geographical unification of the world, the birth of America, the emergence of Prussia and Russia as major European powers, the triumph of capitalism and modern science and their application to agriculture and industry, the formulation of progressive educational and judicial reforms, the rise of the ideas of national sovereignty and inviolable human rights, of liberal and democratic doctrines, of socialism and communism, and of the novel as a leading literary medium. These bonds are so numerous and significant that many, if not most, historians view the last two and a half centuries as forming a single historical unit. Accordingly, the modern sense of forlornness in the face of an "indifferent universe" is explained less by the climate of opinion as such than by these developments which shaped and modified the climate of opinion itself during this time.

Despite the controversial aspects of his thesis, and also because of the considerable truth in it, Becker raised a timely and important question: the validity and feasibility of the Enlightenment tradition in the contemporary world. This question, and not his scholarly thesis as such, is what subsequently aroused so much criticism. For if it were true that "the *philosophes* demolished the City of Saint Augustine only to rebuild it with more up-to-date materials," what could the Enlightenment possibly have to say to modern mankind? Worse still, what were Americans to think of a society whose institutions and official outlook were so deeply rooted in this tradition, yet whose current "climate of opinion" was so incompatible with it? Did this not amount to an "internal contradiction," a sort of inconsistency between ideal and reality which prevents further progress and signalizes a society out of control? The liberal values and mentality of the Enlightenment as embodied in the *American Constitution,* in the *Declaration of the Rights of Man and of the Citizen,* and in the revolutionary credo—liberty, equality, fraternity—were these merely vestiges of the Middle Ages? And the Enlightenment conception of reason as the great integrating force in human life, the faculty which enables man not only to understand the world, but also to change it in accordance with general human needs and aspirations—was this conception obsolete and alien to modern man? In a word, Becker posed the question of where modern man does, can, and should stand in relation to the Enlightenment tradition.

The relationship of the Enlightenment to contemporary society is the point of reference of this book. At the very center of it is the apparent paradox that the triumph of the bourgeoisie, that social class out of which and for which the Enlightenment was conceived, marks the beginning of the decline of the Enlightenment tradition. For the Enlightenment was the creation and ideological expression of the bourgeoisie, which rose to predominance in the eighteenth century and has remained predominant in the advanced areas of the Western world ever since. Yet, the assaults on the Enlightenment tradition have increased in scope and intensity throughout the nineteenth and twentieth centuries, the period of bourgeois hegemony. The line of attack runs from Romanticism and the Restoration through the failure of the liberal uprisings of 1848 and the spread of autocratic, illiberal rule (e.g. Napoleon III and Bismarck) to the age of imperialism and the burgeoning of totalitarianism in our own time. It seems as if the bourgeoisie, once it came to power, lost faith in the very ideals in the name of which it had claimed that power. Many people throughout the nineteenth century, reactionaries and radicals alike, felt that the triumph of "reason" amounted to little more than the triumph of the middle class and that the limitations of the one were reflected in the inadequacies of the other. Becker himself, a liberal in the Enlightenment tradition, only a generation ago noted despairingly that:

> Before the end of the nineteenth century, at all events, it was obvious that the abolition of old oppressions and inequalities had done little more than make room for new ones; and when men realized that democratic government as a reality, as it actually functioned in that besmirched age of iron, was, after all, only another way of being indifferently governed, those once glamorous words, *liberté, égalité, fraternité,* lost their prophetic power for the contented. . . .

The fact that the Enlightenment, the creation of the bourgeoisie in its "heroic age," found itself on the defensive once this class came to power raises crucial questions which make the Enlightenment so problematical for our time: How could this tradition serve the interests of the middle class at one point in its development and not at another? What in it was favorable to specifically bourgeois interests and what indifferent or inimical to them? Conversely, what in the historical development of this class made it receptive to a certain set of ideals at one point and uncomfortable with them at another? Was the Enlightenment nothing more than the ideology of the middle class which could be discarded once this class came to power? Or, even if this be granted, is it not true that every ideology, as a ploy if nothing else, must appeal to universal principles in order to achieve its end? Finally, and more to our present purpose, can we find answers to these questions in the eighteenth century itself? Is there anything in the formative phase of the Enlightenment tradition, anything in the life of the eighteenth-century bourgeoisie, anything in their interconnection which is symptomatic of the future?

Social and Ideological Bases of the Enlightenment

Before the French Revolution the middle class constituted only a minority of the Third Estate, that legal standing assigned to the undifferentiated mass of the people. But during the eighteenth century the middle class was in fact the one and only progressive social class and capitalism—the unrestricted private use of capital for profit—the most advanced economic system possible. Almost all the opponents of the bourgeoisie and capitalism throughout the century were in one way or another unrealistic and impractical; either reactionary, like the Duc de Saint-Simon, or utopian, like Rousseau, or romantic, like Novalis. Kant, on the other hand, who was almost alone among the leading German thinkers of the period in approving of the French Revolution to the end, was progressive *for his time* when he wrote in his essay "Perpetual Peace" (1795):

The spirit of commerce, which is incompatible with war, sooner or later gains the upper hand in every state. As the power of money is perhaps the most dependable of all the powers (means) included under the state power, states see themselves forced, without any moral urge, to promote honorable peace and by mediation to prevent war wherever it threatens to break out.

Before the French Revolution there was only one progressive world-view of any significance, the rationalistic and humanistic Enlightenment. Its spokesmen, who were concentrated in just those countries where the middle class was strongest, France and England, were the formulators of the main current of the Enlightenment: classical liberalism. They believed in human progress, or at least in the possibility of it. They believed in the ability of reason to promote progress and distrusted irrational doctrines and institutions, especially tradition and revealed religion. Following the lead of science, which had made tremendous advances during the seventeenth century, they tended to be materialistic in outlook and empirical in approach. "Reason always consists in seeing things as they are," we read in Voltaire's *Philosophical Dictionary* (1764). "Dare to know!" Kant urged in his essay "What is Enlightenment?" (1784). A kind of realistic rationalism pervades the Enlightenment tradition, the "essential articles" of which Becker enumerates as follows:

(1) man is not natively depraved; (2) the end of life is life itself, the good life on earth instead of the beatific life after death; (3) man is capable, guided solely by the light of reason and experience, of perfecting the good life on earth; and (4) the first and essential condition of the good life on earth is the freeing of men's minds from the bonds of ignorance and superstition, and of their

bodies from the arbitrary oppression of the constituted social authorities.

But "guided solely by the light of reason and experience," how could "the first and essential condition of the good life on earth" be effected? For the enlighteners, who were nearly always concerned with political and social reform, it was a question above all of opposing in one way or another the still semifeudal and ecclesiastical Old Regime. In the concrete historical situation, however, this entailed championing the establishment of a bourgeois social order. For while they appealed to values and principles which are universal in scope, such as rule by law, the equality of all before the law, basic human rights, freedom of thought and expression—in a word, life, liberty, and the pursuit of happiness—they did so quite naturally in terms of the specific interests of the most progressive social class of the time and the one from which most of them sprang. In assigning to the middle class the task of realizing the "good life on earth," they tended to equate it with the good life of this class.

Accordingly, classical liberalism visualized the human world as an agglomeration of autonomous individuals each seeking his own self-interest by increasing his pleasures and decreasing his pains. Society was thought of as a body of equal competitors who entered into contractual relations with one another if their individual interests would be mutually served thereby. The social good represented the arithmetical sum of individual goods. The proper aim of society was to provide for the greatest happiness of the greatest number, a notion which Jeremy Bentham (1748–1832) made the main tenet of utilitarianism. It is true that, for classical liberalism, "self-interest" might include benevolence. However, this was not a peculiarly moral or social duty, but simply another way of bringing happiness to the individual. As Baron d'Holbach, who was a representative exponent of this view, wrote in his *System of Nature* (1770), "Interest is nothing but what each of us considers necessary for his happiness."

First among the things that brought happiness was private property. John Locke (1632–1704), foremost of the classical liberals, claimed that this was the most basic natural right, while Adam Smith provided this "natural" right with a theoretical justification in his *Wealth of Nations* (1776), the outstanding application of classical liberalism to economics. Smith attempted to show that the competitive pursuit of self-interest, if not interfered with, not only results in a "natural" social order, but also leads to a rapid increase of wealth, which was assumed to be the best way to bring about the greatest happiness of the greatest number. The social division of labor was the basis of his system, and he claimed that the division of labor would operate best (*i.e.* in the interest of everyone, including the workers) if the means of production, the accumulation of capital, and its reinvestment were all in private hands. Capitalism, therefore, was as "natural" as progress and the best way to promote it. The most progressive world-view of the eighteenth century was thus made to correspond with the values, interests, and actual behavior of the most progressive social class of the time.

But the growing influence of capitalism and the materialistic ideology that went with it seemed to result in what the leading Jacobin revolutionary, Maximilien Robespierre (1758–1794), summed up as a "practical philosophy which, reducing selfishness to a system, looks on human society as the battle-ground of cunning, which measures right and wrong by the yard-stick of success, which regards probity as a matter of taste or decorum, and the world as the heritage of the astute egoist." By Robespierre's time, in fact, it seemed to some that the humanism of the Enlightenment was not after all compatible with specifically bourgeois values and the competitive, *laissez-faire* economic system. In the early nineteenth century, the liberal, David Ricardo, in his *Principles of Political Economy* (1817), uncovered some unpleasant internal errors in Smith's system, and capitalism produced such widespread misery as the century progressed that political economy came to be known as the "dismal" science. But the Enlightenment itself already manifests a nascent discord between its universal human ideal and the emerging bourgeois social reality. The chief problem facing the enlighteners, in their sincere effort to realize the "good life on earth," was to reconcile the citizen and the bourgeois in man. Robert Mauzi, in his recent work on the Enlightenment, sums up the situation thus:

> The eighteenth century fluctuated between two poles, one bourgeois, the other heroic (whether it was the heroism of reason, the imagination, or of feeling). It seems that the great problem was to arrive at an absolute at no matter what price (whence the heroism); then to ensconce and maintain it in its most steadfast and reassuring form, to change it into a *dictate* which no longer could be eluded (whence the bourgeois degradation). A more amazing mixture of temerity and wariness, of lucidity and illusion cannot be conceived. (*L' Idée du Bonheur dans la Littérature et la Pensée Francaise au XVIII Siècle.*)

Beginning with Rousseau, the bourgeoisie itself became subject to serious criticism, and this criticism grew more vociferous in the last quarter of the eighteenth century. It was during its final phase, especially in Germany, that the fluctuation of the Enlightenment between the heroic and the bourgeois reached its peak. Its heroic side came to fruition in the humanistic ideal of the citizen living in self-fulfilling harmony with himself and with society. This ideal informs the political theories of Montesquieu and Rousseau, Voltaire's campaign on behalf of reason, justice, and tolerance, Diderot's dialectical approach to nature and society, Pestalozzi's views on education, Beccaria's proposals for penal reform, Kant's philosophy of practical reason, the new historical conception of Herder, and the aesthetic ideals of Lessing and Goethe.

The bourgeois side of the Enlightenment took the form of a revised version of the medieval notion of a "hidden hand," according to which a basic but unseen harmony underlies the apparent discord of the world. To the middle-class enlighteners, the "hidden hand" was that invisible force which would make public virtue, the citizen in man, result necessarily and automatically from private self-seeking. This view can be found in various forms in Mandeville, Pope, in deism, in the *laissez-faire* economic doctrine of the Physiocrats and Adam Smith, in the mechanistic-utilitarian social theory of the encyclopedists, in Leibniz's teaching of the preestablished harmony of the universe, and in the idealistic aspect of Kant's philosophy.

Throughout the century, the heroic and the bourgeois sides of the Enlightenment confronted and constantly counteracted each other. For the belief in a "hidden hand," whether expressed as naturalistic determinism or as idealistic determinism, is a metaphysical belief, which implies a fatalism that is inimical to humanism. If man is solely the product of natural necessity, or subject to an inaccessible, unknowable reality beyond nature, he cannot be the creator and master of a rationally ordered human world; he becomes rather the plaything of influences and forces beyond his control. Nature and reason, thus conceived, evaporate into abstractions and can no longer serve as the basis for a feasible doctrine of human freedom. This undercurrent of fatalism prevented the enlighteners from working out a theory of action which could serve to translate their humanistic ideal into reality. Underlying this dilemma were the inconsistencies of bourgeois life itself before the French Revolution. Hence, the social and historical setting of the Enlightenment will be our point of departure in considering its fluctuation between the heroic and the bourgeois.

ABSOLUTE MONARCHY AND CLASS CONFLICT IN THE EIGHTEENTH CENTURY

"This has been a century of vile bourgeoisie," noted the Duc de Saint-Simon (1675–1755) in 1715, the year in which Louis XIV died. A gossip, a crank, but a sharp observer and critic of court life in the closing decades of the Sun King's reign, Saint-Simon was an embittered witness to the systematic exclusion of his class from the political life of France and its reduction to a parasitic, sycophantic existence at Versailles. He was quite right to see the degradation of the nobility as part of Louis' policy of shifting political responsibility to bourgeois ministers, like Colbert and Louvois, and of enabling bourgeois to enter into political life through the practice of venality (the sale of public offices). Pressed by the need to finance the con-

tinual warfare and extravagance that marked the final decades of his reign, Louis also was motivated to adopt this
policy by the memory of the Fronde (1648–1652), when
bourgeois and aristocrats momentarily joined forces against
the crown. Determined that such a collaboration should
never recur, Louis always took care to set the one class
against the other and, by preserving an equilibrium between them, to hold decisive power in his own hands. The
wisdom of this policy lay in the fact that for the time being
it prevented from happening in France what had recently
happened in England: namely, the overthrow of royal absolutism and the creation of a social and political order in
which, as the observer, Rabaud Saint-Étienne, expressed it,
"nation and king would be nothing, the aristocrats would
be everything." This policy had its Achilles heel, however.
Whereas the English aristocracy had sacrificed some of its
privileges in order to maintain and augment its power,
Louis, in depriving the French nobility of its power, ap-
peased them by allowing them to retain their privileges.

But with the death of Louis, and with his successor
still in his minority, a political vacuum was created, and an
opportunity to reverse this policy at long last presented
itself. The retention of privileges as a *legal* right, the right
that distinguished the French from the English aristocracy
at this time, would serve as the basis for that resurgence of
the nobility so ardently urged by Saint-Simon. Although
the desire for such a resurgence was only one of a number
of long-suppressed forces which came to the surface in
1715—others being the parlements, Gallicanism, a powerful
business class, and an overtaxed and oppressed peasantry—
it proved to be in the long run the most decisive one for
French political life. For by 1780 the nobility had effectively
foiled the crown's efforts at reform. It had ruined the leading

reform ministers, Maupeou (1714–1792) and Turgot (1727–1781), gained control of all the high clerical offices of the realm, and monopolized the military. Thus as Franklin Ford has pointed out, if the French nobility "did not have the strength to suppress revolution, [it] had at least recovered enough strength to make revolution inevitable."

Throughout the century there persisted the idea of the reform of society by the aristocracy. The Baron de Montesquieu (1689–1755) regarded the aristocracy as the one class which could prevent the degeneration of monarchy into despotism. Fénelon, Saint-Simon, Boulainvilliers, and others of the old aristocracy, in their reactionary yearnings, hearkened back to the early Middle Ages when the Frankish conquerors, forming an aristocratic leadership, supplanted centralized authority. Mirabeau opposed royal encroachments of any kind. The chevalier d'Arc advocated the revival of a military caste, and Vauvenargues, a sort of heroic cult of glory. Above all, there was the ever present example of England where the aristocracy ruled the country. In taking this reactionary stand against royal absolutism, the nobility prepared the way for its own downfall. According to John Lough, "One of the paradoxes of eighteenth-century French history is that the Revolution, which was to sweep away the privileges of the nobility and to destroy its political power, was largely precipitated by that very section of the community."

In Central and Eastern Europe, in Prussia, Russia, and the Habsburg Empire, absolutism grew steadily stronger in the course of the century. Frederick the Great (1740–1786), Catherine the Great (1762–1796), and Joseph II (1780–1790) made more or less successful efforts to integrate the aristocracy with the apparatus of state and to establish fairly efficient and loyal bureaucracies. In contrast to these countries, where no strong middle class existed, and where the effects of the Enlightenment were more superficial than in France, and in contrast to England, where under the inept Hanoverians power came to center in the national Parliament, the French monarchy gradually and unevenly but irrevocably succumbed to the feudal resurgence. Louis XIV had embodied and carried to its extreme the theory of the divine right of kings. His rule was based on the threefold theory of the supreme power of the Roman emperor, a conception revived during the Renaissance; on the medieval notion of dominion, according to which the realm was considered to be the patrimony of the feudal lord; and on the divine authority traditionally ascribed to a Christian prince for which the Bible provided support. But even during Louis' reign, the leading Catholic cleric of France and spokesman for his rule, the Bishop Bossuet (1627–1704), felt impelled, in his refutation of the Huguenot Jurieu's attack on the theory of divine right, to resort to Hobbes' argument of utility, contending that absolutism alone promotes the welfare of the people. The utilitarian justification for despotism advanced by Thomas Hobbes (1588–1679) was taken up by the enlightened reform statesmen of the eighteenth century. It was also supported, until Rousseau, by most of the leading enlighteners, who were, with the significant exceptions of Montesquieu and Holbach, men of the middle class: Voltaire the son of a notary, Grimm the son of a pastor, Diderot of a cutler, and Rousseau of a watchmaker.

But if utility can be used as an argument in favor of absolutism, it can also be turned against it once the despot fails to provide for the welfare of the population, or once there ceases to be common agreement about what constitutes the welfare of society. Even if individuals find themselves organized in a higher social unity when they agree, by means of a contract, on an absolute ruler, Hobbes' theory still does not provide for a metamorphosis of the individual or community will. That is, his theory does not take history into account. In this very weakness, however, lies its historical importance, for under changing conditions it implies the feasibility of revolution as a means to bring about a social order more in accordance with utility conceived in a new way. Thus, a seed of revolution was planted in France by royal absolutism itself at its very zenith, a seed that would later contribute to the overthrow of both royal absolutism and aristocracy.

Throughout most of the eighteenth century, however, hostility to privilege and tradition was confined in fact to a small intelligentsia. As long as rulers encountered no general opposition to their policies, as long as they could maintain a degree of public order and squeeze enough money from their subjects to maintain their courts and armies, they actually showed little interest in reforming their states along utilitarian lines. More often than not enlightened reforms were adopted only to enforce absolutism. The typical eighteenth-century state was a *Herrenstaat*, a state governed by and for the interests of the feudal aristocracy. Its guiding principle was not the welfare of the people, but rather the preservation and increase of the power of the state. This principle required a constant strengthening of the state's position in a system of other ruthlessly competitive *Herrenstaaten*. It was inevitable in such a system, with its incessant rivalries, the constant pressure brought to bear on each individual state, and the unremitting attention required by the military machine, that warfare would be the ultimate court of appeal. In a system based on international rivalry (which is what the balance of power then amounted to), what else but war could test the strength of a state? We need only recall the periods of general warfare during this time: 1689–1713, 1740–1748, 1756–1763, 1776–1783, and 1792–1815. It was war that established Prussia and Russia as powers to be reckoned with, war that brought about the birth of America and the decline of Sweden and the Ottoman Empire as major powers, war that substituted Spanish for Austrian influence in southern Italy, made Lorraine a French province, and helped Britain establish a great colonial empire.

The Seven Years War (1756–1763) broke up the old balance of power in which Bourbon had been pitted against Habsburg (the so-called Diplomatic Revolution of midcentury) and initiated a period of political and diplomatic confusion, while the emergence of Prussia and Russia on the scene and the revival of Habsburg power increased the tension. France and England fought each other constantly both in Europe and abroad in a series of struggles sometimes called the Second Hundred Years War. The new importance of overseas expansion is attested by the fact that England emerged as the leading European power without acquiring any territory on the continent, except Gibraltar. In 1758 the first serious critic of the balance of power idea, Johann H. G. von Justi (1705–1771), argued that the real criterion of a country's strength is the efficiency of its government, not the extent of its territory, nor even its ability to wage war. He claimed, moreover, that if the balance of power were to be really effective in preventing the excessive growth of a state, it must sooner or later allow for intervention in the internal affairs of the country in question. Indeed, in the course of the century, the dismemberment of a state came to be accepted by diplomats as legitimate procedure, being regarded as a means of "preventive warfare" which was no longer necessarily related to the question of succession, or even to rival territorial claims. The noted French historian, Albert Sorel, sums up the political situation thus: "International law was ruined by the abuse of its own principle. There was no other penalty, but this sufficed, being both fatal and implacable. Because the state was confused with the person of the sovereign, and sovereignty was transmitted by heredity in most states, conflicts over succession became conflicts between states."

One reason why the spate of plans for universal peace put forward in the eighteenth century, from the Abbé de Saint-Pierre (1658–1743) to Immanuel Kant (1724–1804), were without effect is that they failed to take into account this logical result of the raw balance of power system—with "its own jurisprudence: to keep an even balance"; with "its own procedure and formulas, which were those of shyster lawyers, such as the pledging of property to guarantee the completion of a deal"; and with "its own slang, which was that of pawnbrokers, such as margins to safeguard against fluctuations in value, and sureties to make good losses on loans" (Sorel). These plans, which presupposed the stability of the territorial status quo, appeared unrealistic to an age which witnessed Russia's conquest of a Baltic coastline and acquisition of a foothold on the Black Sea, Frederick the Great's legally groundless attacks on Silesia and Saxony, the turning of North America and India into spheres of conflict between England and France, and the partitions of Poland (about which Frederick said that Maria Theresa wept but took her share). Rousseau scarcely exaggerated when he wrote in 1774: "I see all the states of Europe rushing headlong to ruin; monarchies, republics, all those nations whose origins are so glorious and whose governments were built up with so much wisdom, are falling into decay and are threatened by an imminent death. All the great nations are moaning, crushed by their own weight." Under the impact of these developments, along with the growing isolation of Britain from European affairs and the increasing financial insolvency and declining military prestige of France, Europe began to manifest a nostalgia for the innocence and simplicity of a golden age (usually mythical), such as we find in some of the writings of Rousseau and Herder, and also the first stirrings of a "folk" or "cultural" nationalism. The abuse by sovereigns of the prevailing principle of international law paved the way for revolution by holding up an example of political conduct which eventually would be used against these sovereigns themselves.

It is within this context that the Regency (1715–1723) marks a major turning point in French history. For not only was the practical problem of the transference and utilization of power posed in France for the first time in more than fifty years, but there existed now also the theoretical problem of the very nature and source of authority itself. The brilliant philosopher and mathematician, Blaise Pascal (1623–1662), had aptly described and exposed the real basis of authority in seventeenth-century France when he observed: "Custom is the whole of equity and the sole reason for its acceptance; it is the mystical foundation of authority. He who brings equity back to its principle, destroys authority." The question for eighteenth-century French thinkers and statesmen was whether custom would continue to serve as the mystical foundation of authority, or whether there would be an effort to restore equity to its principle. During and after the Regency there was general agreement that the monarchy must be reformed. But whether it should become a positive force for the general good (the theory of enlightened despotism urged by the advocates of social progress, at least until Rousseau), or whether it should become a limited monarchy protecting the privileged (the position of those in support of the feudal resurgence)—that was the issue. In either case, the crown could not continue as an autonomous and dominant political force. First and foremost this meant that the Sun King's policy of preserving an equilibrium between nobility and bourgeoisie was finished. This in turn cleared the field for a direct confrontation of these two classes in a struggle for total power; a confrontation that by the 1780s turned into a collision, with the crown powerless to intervene. As Kingsley Martin said, "The calling of the Estates General [in 1789] was more than a confession that the government needed popular support; it was also an acknowledgment of the people's right to give or withhold it." The whole situation was highly favorable to the emergence of an energetic and effective intelligentsia.

The most important action taken by the Regent, Philip of Orleans (1674–1723), was to restore the right of remonstrance to the parlements, as this proved to be the key move in the feudal resurgence. The parlements were judicial bodies whose function it was to register royal edicts, but whose right it was to refuse registering them if they were not in accordance with divine, natural, and positive law. Bourgeois in origin, emphasizing the virtues of austerity, industry, and thrift, the parlements had helped Henry of Navarre restore order in France after the Wars of Religion, and in so doing, had helped the crown in its struggle for ascendancy over the nobility. With Louis XIV, however, absolutism became an accomplished fact, and the right of remonstrance, with the potential power of resistance to the crown it entailed, was more of a nuisance to him than an aid. Philip's authorization to remonstrate was intended to win back the much needed support of these influential bodies by reversing Louis' policy of circumventing and suppressing them.

Due to the practice of venality in obtaining membership in the parlements, a practice encouraged by Louis XIV himself to raise money, a new aristocracy of wealth and office emerged among these bourgeois magistrates who, though opposed by the hereditary aristocracy, nevertheless tended to identify their interests with it. Montesquieu, who was president of the Bordeaux parlement, defended venality precisely because it contributed to the formation of an intermediate social stratum which would be beyond the reach of king and bourgeois supporters of enlightened monarchy alike. And, as the century progressed, the parlements did in fact increasingly resist reform or proposals for reform of any sort from any quarter. They opposed the crown's attempts at tax reform and any encroachments on feudal and local privileges. They opposed the papal bull of 1713, Unigenitus, and later the ultramontane policies of the ministers Dubois and Fleury, not only because the parlements were against papal interference in French affairs, but mainly because these policies were supported by the crown. They defended Jansenism and the so-called Gallican liberties not only out of religious and national feeling, but because these policies were opposed by the crown. The parlements resisted fiscal reform because the liquidation of offices would threaten their own existence. As an increasing number of members of the parlements became rentiers, they opposed any reduction of rent rates. As more of them purchased titles of nobility, they opposed any royal incursions on seigneurial prerogatives. Along with members of the old aristocracy, like Fénelon, Saint-Simon, and Boulainvilliers, these parvenus increasingly committed themselves to the Germanist theory of French history, according to which the coming of the Franks constituted a cleavage with Roman imperial traditions, as against the Romanist theory, espoused by d'Argenson and Du Bos, according to which the feudal age and the era of the Estates General (a feudal body which had not convened since 1614) represented merely an interruption of proper relations between king and magistracy. "The story of the resurgence of the French nobility is first and foremost the story of how the high robe was to demonstrate its power to obstruct the monarchy and win general recognition as an indispensable defender of privileged interests" (Ford).

As early as the middle of the century most of the magistrates already shared in the exclusionist, reactionary, and selfish class attitude of the old French nobility. The expulsion of the Jesuits from France in 1764, who were the only serious contenders of the magistrates for influence on the crown, and whose downfall the parlements were instrumental in effecting, increased the prestige of the parlements. So too did the king's growing dependence on them to register new and burdensome edicts of taxation necessitated by France's military defeats after mid-century and by the crown's inability and unwillingness to tax the nobility and clergy. In both cases the parlements won popular support, with the result that: "The lawyers found themselves in the odd position of a body of privileged aristocrats, totally hostile to all Liberal reform, upholding the Constitution of France against the Monarch amid the enthusiastic applause of a populace who looked upon them as the champions of liberty and described them as true Romans and Fathers of their country" (Martin).

So popular and successful was their opposition to the crown in the second half of the century that only three years after their suppression in 1771 by Louis XV's reform minister Maupeou, Louis XVI thought it politic to reinstate them. As early as the sixties the lawyer and political observer, Edmond J. F. Barbier, noted in his diary: "If the government succeeds in diminishing the authority and accepted rights of the parlements, there will no longer be any obstacle in the way of assured despotism. If, on the contrary, the parlements unite to oppose this move with strong measures, nothing can follow but a general revolution." And as late as 1776, only thirteen years before the Revolution would sweep away all feudal privileges, the remonstrances still defended these privileges almost in their entirety. With the dismissal of Turgot in 1776 and the resignation of Necker in 1781, all hope of peaceful reform within the existing institutional framework seemed at an end. Only in 1789, when the magistrates chose to stand with the nobility against the Third Estate in the matter of voting procedure,* did the popularity of the parlements crumble. "The fact that the privileged orders were, like the monarchy, the victims of the Revolution, should not be allowed to hide their part in the slow but continuous disintegration of absolutism between 1715 and 1789, a process which began under the Regency of Philippe d' Orléans with the sudden appearance of the aristocracy on the political scene . . . ,

---

* In May 1789, when the Estates General convened for the first time since 1614, the magistrates agreed with the nobility that the three estates, nobility, clergy, and the mass of the population, should vote separately, thus giving the first two estates the power of veto over the third. What the Third Estate wanted was an increase in the number of its representatives to correspond with the increase in size and importance of the middle class, and an assembly in which the three estates would vote together by head.

and then in the infinitely more dangerous revival of the power of the parlements" (Lough).

However, this pattern of development, whereby the parlements in the very process of fusing with the nobility succumbed to its standards, is not a unique phenomenon in history. Rising classes often tend to identify with formerly dominant groups, with their tastes, values, attitudes, and conduct. The result is that this carry-over into the present of heritages deemed desirable often arrests their natural erosion by evolution. Some examples of this pattern are the ancient Roman *Equites*, the German *ministeriales* after the Investiture Struggle, the fifteenth-century Florentine patriciate, and the nineteenth-century German bureaucrats, about whom the distinguished German scholar, Fritz Kern, obseved: "That battle of officialdom against the feudal aristocracy was seriously hindered by the ever more threatening merger of officeholders and old nobility." As we shall see, a similar fusion of courtly and middle-class ideals also took place in eighteenth-century Germany, though not so completely as in France, since Germany lacked a politically effective bourgeois force comparable to the French parlements.

The restoration of the right of the parlements to remonstrate created another condition favorable to the emergence of a vigorous and critical bourgeois intelligentsia. For the principle to which the parlements appealed in their remonstrances was that of a contract between king and people which, if violated, implied the right of the people to resist and, if necessary, to revolt. If, in reality, the parlements ceased to represent the people, the principle was still acknowledged by all. The "merger of officeholders [in this case, the only bourgeois elements that carried any political

weight] and old aristocracy" altered radically the constella-
tion of social forces in France, so that "in place of the seventeenth-century's characteristic triangle—the crown, the
sword, and the still half-bourgeois robe—there now appeared a triangle composed of the crown, the middle-class
reformers, and the noble defenders of existing privileges
based on birth and office" (Ford). The *philosophes* generally supported the reformers. Voltaire, for one, protested
the king's abolition of Maupeou's new parlements "which
had always known how to obey," and his reinstatement of
the old ones "which had done nothing but defy him." This
social re-ordering brought about by the evolution of the
parlements provides some insights into the "vile bourgeoisie"
about whom Saint-Simon spoke in 1715, and how it is that
the parlements could count on their support for so long.

The Third Estate comprised the vast majority of the
population, all elements exclusive of the clergy and nobility.
As the term estate applied mainly to the legal status of the
various social classes, and as the peasantry, the middle class
and the still nascent working class shared the same legal
status, no distinction was made between them. Indeed,
since the feudal structure of society was inimical to the
interests of all these groups, they had a common interest in
opposing and finally overthrowing it. Only with the
French Revolution and the fall of feudalism did the term
"estate" become obsolete and the divergency of interests of
the groups formerly comprising the Third Estate become
apparent.

As distinguished from the peasantry and the working
class, the bourgeoisie was that social group whose interests
and functions were bound up with capitalism, which was
then in its commercial phase. The competitive character of
capitalism stimulated a constant rationalization of the

means of production. Seventeenth-century mercantilism, the economic contribution to early state-making, had given a tremendous impetus to capitalism, and throughout the eighteenth century the need to improve all aspects of the state, so as to enable it to maintain and improve its position in a competitive political system, continued to encourage the rationalization of economic life. Improved production stimulated a growth in population. Between 1700 and 1800 the population of France rose from about 20 to 26 million, that of the Habsburg Empire from about 20 to 27 million, and that of England from about 5.5 to 9 million. This population increase meant a greater demand for goods both within Europe and in the expanding colonial areas. Since the most rapid growth of population occurred in England, which also had the most extensive colonial empire, it is not surprising that England took the lead in mechanizing industry. These conditions, coupled with the pressure of constant warfare, required ever greater productivity; greater productivity demanded greater rationalization of production which acted in turn as a stimulus to the advancement of capitalism. Before the end of the century, commercial capitalism gave way to the more productive phase of industrial capitalism, with England making dramatic advances in the textile, metal, and power industries. The important stages in this transition have been summarized as follows:

> First, this demand [for more goods] was in many cases concentrated at ports and cities and could not be met by village handicraftsmen. Therefore producers were encouraged to seek means to increase supply. Second, the supply of some products like linen was relatively inelastic (that is, could not readily be increased to satisfy demand). Thus entrepreneurs were led to seek substitute products such as cotton. Third, prices began to go up by the second quarter of the eighteenth century, so that producers

had an extra incentive to turn out more goods. Finally, the population boom resulted in a shortage of employment opportunities on the land and gave rise to a group of labor which was in search of work and not adverse to moving into towns and factories. It provided the available labor supply which was essential to the Industrial Revolution. (Clough, S. B. et al. *Early Modern Times*, p. 659.)

Advances in agriculture also contributed, at least in England, to the growth of capitalism. Landlords there "enclosed" land—cleared it of the peasants who had traditionally cultivated it for their own use—so that the landlords themselves might grow marketable crops on it. Stimulated by the incentive for profit, they introduced new crops and improved techniques of cultivation. By contrast, in France, and in much of continental Europe, landlords continued to depend for income on traditional feudal dues from the peasantry. (In areas like East Prussia, southern Italy, and southern Spain, where agriculture was in fact organized along capitalist lines in great *latifundia,* the peasantry was kept bound to the soil partly because there existed no thriving commercial or industrial centers to which they could migrate, and no strong middle class with which they could pool their resources in opposing feudal exploitation.) In order to meet inflation, French landlords sought to extract larger payments from the peasants and thus incurred their hostility. This peasant discontent was one of the precipitating factors of the Revolution, and probably the most immediate one. The middle-class economic reformers, known as the Physiocrats, tried to extend capitalism to agriculture and impose a single land tax on an economically reactivated aristocratic landowning class, a plan which might have stimulated a development in

France similar to that taking place in England. But the efforts of the Physiocrats were largely in vain due to the vitality of feudalism in France, especially the socially divisive legal barriers, which discouraged the nobility from engaging in any productive economic activity whatever.

The feudal social structure of France favored the growth of the bourgeoisie in another way also. In the course of its resurgence the French nobility, with its traditional contempt for work and commerce, but pressed from below by the rising middle class, gained a monopoly on the political and military life of the country. This monopoly, based of course on social inequality, had the effect of polarizing bourgeoisie and nobility still further. Since eighteenth-century technology still allowed for "limited" warfare, and since total mobilization therefore was neither necessary nor desired by governments eager to protect the productive sources of their military might (Frederick the Great thought that battles were best fought without the knowledge of the civilian population), this legal inequality could be maintained and fortified. The bourgeoisie could be excluded from the "heroic" task of warfare, which was the traditional preserve and practically the only remaining justification for existence of the aristocracy, and confined to the merely economic function of production. The middle-class enlighteners reacted by debunking the aristocracy's heroic scale of values, claiming that economic utility was the true criterion of virtue. Voltaire typified this bourgeois reaction:

> I will not take it upon me to say which is the most useful to his country, and which of the two ought to have the preference; whether the powdered lord, who knows to a minute when the king rises or goes to bed, perhaps to stool, and who gives himself airs of importance in playing the part of a slave in the antechamber of some minister;

or the merchant who enriches his country, . . . thereby
contributing to the happiness and convenience of human
nature. (*Letters on the English.*)

What aroused the wrath of the enlighteners was not
so much the aristocracy's way of life as such, nor even its
privileges, but rather that its privileged way of life no
longer seemed to be justified by its actual functions. According to Alexis de Tocqueville in his classic, *The Old
Regime and the French Revolution* (1856): "We are fully
justified in saying that the very destruction of some of the
institutions of the Middle Ages made those which survived
seem all the more detestable" (Bk. II, chap. 1). In the
process of berating the aristocracy, the enlighteners naturally tended to set up the utilitarian principle of bourgeois
existence as a universal value. It was a case of one action
producing an equal but opposite reaction. If the nobility
had little other justification for existence than its traditional
ideal of heroism, the bourgeoisie had no other ideal than
its unheroic existence. If the aristocratic ideal of heroism
substituted for economic and social usefulness, bourgeois
usefulness was elevated into a heroic ideal. The bourgeois
debunking of aristocratic ideology thus contributed to what
Hans Speier has called the "modern reversal of the old
relationship between the 'utile,' the 'honestum,' and the
'summum bonum.' "

By the eighteenth century, capitalism had reached
the point where money ceased to be merely a means of exchange and became a form of bourgeois property. That is,
it acted as a solvent of the old social order, vying with and
steadily superseding feudal property, such as hereditary
land and privileges. The sale of offices and titles increased
so that distinctions of wealth tended to supplant those of
birth. The social effect of capitalism in England, where

legal barriers separating the classes no longer existed, was to bring the landed aristocracy and merchant class closer together. Far from making the British aristocracy bourgeois, however, this merger enabled it to preserve its peculiar way of life and outlook and to maintain its position as the politically dominant class well into the nineteenth century. In France, the advance of capitalism had the effect of sharpening the cleavage between the classes. The limited social mobility that did exist merely tended to promote stratification within the classes themselves. On the one hand, as we have seen, a plutocracy emerged within the bourgeoisie which sought to buy its way into the aristocracy, thereby separating itself from the rest of this class. On the other hand, this process undermined the security and self-confidence of the old aristocracy which sought to disassociate itself from these upstarts. "As a reaction against the parvenu who was flaunting his title of baron or marquis, the genuine old nobility were signing their names only, while the masked ball is the typical Parisian divertissement of a class with an uneasy conscience, clinging to privileges it has ceased to believe in" (J. McManners). And, during the decade preceding the Revolution: "Balloons, mesmerism, scientific discovery, a vague humanitarianism and the 'simple life' had become the vogue among the aristocracy" (Martin).

The importance of the middle class and capitalism for eighteenth-century history lies precisely in the fact that they did not yet dominate all aspects of society, but rather were becoming the dominant social and economic forces in a society which was in all other respects still semifeudal. The result was increasing discord between these forces and the political life, institutions, and ideology of society. As a rising social class, the bourgeoisie found itself torn between a desire to identify with the traditionally dominant nobility and loyalty to its own utilitarian outlook raised to the level of a universal value. The originally bourgeois parlements simply carried the first tendency to its extreme. But this tension, this "ambivalence in bourgeois class attitudes between adherence to the traditional system and the expectation of mobility . . . based on universalistic values" (Elinor Barber), helps to explain why for so long the middle class was inclined to support the parlements which had become by mid-century bodies of privileged aristocrats. It also helps to explain the general tendency of the bourgeois until late in the century "to fly away as quickly as possible from socially despised commerce into occupations that carried greater social prestige" (Barber).

So long as the common political front formed by the privileged orders and the Third Estate against the crown lasted—a common front in which the nobility took the initiative—the bourgeoisie continued to share, though to an ever decreasing extent, the adherence of the nobility to the "traditional system." So long as the bourgeoisie was torn by an ambivalent social attitude, it remained politically paralyzed and passive, (a condition particularly characteristic of Germany and one which greatly influenced its intellectual and artistic output). Even in France, however, it was not until the common front collapsed in the eighties, when the conflict of interests between the privileged orders and the Third Estate became generally apparent, that the social outlook of the bourgeoisie ceased to be ambivalent. What made the bourgeoisie so vile in the eyes of the acutely class-conscious Saint-Simon was just the fact that, though undeserving in its unheroic, opportunistic style of life, it was nonetheless in 1715 the only "potentially mobile group" in society. It remained so as long as channels were kept open to its members to acquire noble status. Only as the successful feudal resurgence put an end to this social mobility did the bourgeoisie become decisively revolutionary in outlook, as exemplified by the hero of Beaumarchais' *Marriage of Figaro* (1784):

> Monsieur le Comte. Because you are a great noblemen, you think yourself a great genius! Nobility, fortune, rank position: all these make one so proud! What have you done to win so many advantages? You have taken the trouble to be born, and nothing more! For the rest, you are a man ordinary enough! While, as for me, lost in the obscure crowd, I have had to use more knowledge and planning merely to exist than have been expended over the last hundred years in governing all of Spain. (Act V, 3.)

THE
ENLIGHTENMENT
AS CULTURAL
REVOLUTION:
ORIGINS

As late as 1748, however, little change was apparent on the surface of French society. Church and state seemed as stable and secure as ever. The king was still popular after a successful war, and the parlements and Jansenists had as yet made little headway in their struggle against absolutism and the Jesuits. The Enlightenment was not yet a coherent movement, but only a conception taking shape in the minds of a scattered handful of individual thinkers, writers, and social critics. Nothing at this time suggested that the Old Regime could not continue to maintain itself. But, as we have seen, decisive social and political regroupings were in process between 1715 and 1748. Then in 1748 appeared Montesquieu's *The Spirit of the Laws*, Hume's *Inquiry Concerning Human Understanding*, La Mettrie's *Man a Machine;* in 1749 Diderot's *Letter on the Blind;* in 1750 Rousseau's first discourse; in 1751 the first volume of the *Encyclopedia;* and in 1755 Morelly's *Code of Nature,* the first modern conception of a communist society. The brief period during which these and many other important writings appeared marks the point at which the forces at work below the surface came to the fore and began to gain the upper hand.

Montesquieu and the Problem of Society

In tracing this early phase of the Enlightenment, we must go back to the greatest literary work of the Regency. Montesquieu's *The Persian Letters* (1721), the first great writing of the first great *philosophe.* A sharp, satirical criticism of contemporary France, it continued the spirit of seventeenth-century philosophy. Descartes' rationalism, Locke's empiricism, the scepticism of Pierre Bayle, all contributed to the undermining of men's confidence in the past as a guide to action in the present. "If, now, men turned their backs on the past," writes Paul Hazard, "it was because they thought it something evanescent, Protean, something impossible to grasp and retain, something inherently and inveterately deceptive." This loss of confidence in history, while it paved the way for the Enlightenment doctrine of progress, also generated widespread scepticism and cynicism between 1680 and 1715. The so-called Quarrel between the Ancients and Moderns, which dominated this period of transition from seventeenth- to eighteenth-century European intellectual life, was symptomatic of this new spirit. For the issue as to whether human culture had progressed since antiquity was not merely an academic literary dispute; it was grounded rather in conflicting attitudes toward the cultural policy of royal absolutism. The element of the

bourgeoisie favored by mercantilism and political centralization in the person of the king generally stood on the side
of the "Moderns," whose leading spokesman was the Cartesian savant, Bernard le Bovier de Fontenelle (1657–1757),
philosopher, playwright, and president of the French Academy of Sciences throughout the first half of the eighteenth
century. This sophisticated and subtle popularizer of science
argued that the accumulation of knowledge and the uniformity of human nature logically meant that modern
civilization was more advanced, or at least not less advanced, than ancient Greco-Roman civilization. Most of the
magistrates and the landowning bourgeois, those who opposed royal absolutism, favored the "Ancients." The "Moderns" won the day, but a few of the more farseeing
disputants, Boileau, La Bruyère, and La Fontaine, who were
typical Parisian burghers, did defend the supremacy of
antiquity as a gesture of resistance to the all-inclusive claims
of the crown. They saw no reason to believe in the limitless
progress of the existing order.

Regency France, and the multitude of petty German
courts which aped the French example, fully justified this
growing cynicism toward the past on the one hand, and
toward the present state of affairs on the other. Political,
economic, and moral confusion prevailed and reinforced
each other. Debauchery and avarice were rampant; shady
financial dealings and arbitrary justice were commonplaces;
scandal and intrigue ruled the day. The Regent himself
was a usurper, having put aside the will of Louis XIV,
and a prime exemplar of the burgeoning corruption. The
greatness of *The Persian Letters* lies in the scope of Montesquieu's conception, his grasp of the essentials of a society
in the first throes of disintegration and its crippling effects
on human life and character. The recurrent theme of the

Letters is the dehumanization of man by and through all the institutions of society.

Montesquieu descended from families belonging to both the nobility of the robe and that of the sword (*i.e.* to new and old nobility). While holding to the ideal of limited monarchy on the English model, he wished to see the reactivation of the nobility as the politically responsible class in France. Unlike the old aristocracy, however, he visualized this achievement, not in further exclusionism and retrenchment, but rather in the consolidation of an aristocracy of merit which would cut across the class lines of old and new aristocracy and form a solid front independent of Third Estate and crown alike. He approved of venality, for example, on the grounds that it encouraged trade by holding out the incentive of political reward, permitted the government to make use of business success in private life as a criterion for ennoblement and success in public life, and simultaneously increased the strength and autonomy of the magistracy which would form the backbone of his projected *corps intermédiaires*. Montesquieu suffered setbacks in his personal life, such as disappointment in love and a marriage of convenience to a Protestant commoner, whose dowry helped to restore the sagging family fortune. Like Saint-Simon, whom he admired and whom he personally presented with a copy of his *Thoughts on the Greatness of the Romans and Their Decline* (1734), his hopes for a high political career were frustrated. These setbacks influenced his withdrawal into the world of learning and scholarship, from which vantage point he cultivated his talents as a critical thinker. It seems a paradox that this man, who remained a monarchist, a member of the Catholic Church, and an aristocrat to the core, should have initiated a movement that in the end would sweep away everything in which he believed. But it is precisely as a paradox, as a man in whose life and writings the basic contradictory forces and interests of the age converged in dramatic conflict, that Montesquieu is so historically significant. If he did not solve the problems of the age, he at least recognized and formulated them in a way that eventually could lead to their solution.

The Persian Letters

The Persian Letters was the first attempt in the eighteenth century to discuss serious issues in the form of an epistolary novel. Montesquieu's purpose in adopting this literary form, he relates in "Some Reflections on *The Persian Letters*" (1754), was "to mix philosophy, politics, and ethics into a novel and to bind the whole together by a secret and, so to speak, obscure chain." His intention was to provide the reader with a constantly fresh view on events and to register the immediate reactions of his characters to situations as they happened. Montesquieu wished not merely to discuss issues, but to dramatize them as they are experienced in their living wholeness. The chief advantage of the epistolary novel, in his view, was that "people themselves become aware of their present circumstances, and this makes the passions involved more sensible to the reader than all the third-person reports one could write on the subject."

In the course of the century, the novel of letters, and the philosophical *conte* which grew out of it, became popular everywhere. But too often the former degenerated into a merely stylistic convention, unrelated to what the author wished to say. Too often letters were merely reports of events, written by characters with a seemingly compulsive urge to write letters. It has been calculated, for example, that Richardson's Clarissa must have scribbled away sometimes a good eight hours a day. Too often, and this is a frequent failing of *The Persian Letters*, the letters only tell the story; they do not form an integral part of it as they do in the last great epistolary novel of the century, Laclos' *Les Liaisons Dangereuses* (1782). Before the end of the century, this literary form gave way to the *Bildungsroman*, of which Goethe's *Wilhelm Meister's Apprenticeship* (1796) is the best example. Here the reader confronts, not a series of inactive letter-writers, but pulsating personalities in the process of formation, an artistic approach more in accordance with modern taste. However, before the problem of personality and the problematical personality could become central to the novel, the realization was necessary that the individual is not merely an isolated observer of the world, standing apart from and having no effect on it, but rather is involved in dynamic interaction with the world (a realization finally forced upon the European mind by the French Revolution).

The Persian Letters marks a major step in this direction. The importance of Montesquieu's stylistic innovation, for all of its limitations, is that it is rooted in the actual experiencing of the basic historical realities of the time; and nowhere do the realities of Regency France find better expression than in these letters. Out of the confusion and corruption of the era, which seemed to bear out the maxim of the Cardinal de Retz that "The rights of peoples and the prerogatives of kings never agree so well as in silence," Montesquieu succeeded in depicting the interdependence and immediacy of philosophy, politics, and ethics, and the involvement of the subject with them. The "obscure chain" is the logic hidden behind apparently arbitrary appearances, a logic that emerges as a theory of laws of political decline and "ideal types" in *The Spirit of the Laws*.

Montesquieu, who traveled widely himself, made use of the fast growing literature on geographical discovery, such as Jean Chardin's *Voyages en Perse et aux Indes orientales,* and the new taste for things oriental, as evinced by the recent translation into French of *The Thousand and One Nights*. His spokesman, Usbek, is not only a disinterested observer abroad, who sees things in "strange ways"; he is also a citizen of a distant but real country realistically depicted. Montesquieu moves to and fro between the complex, concrete world of contemporary Europe and the remote, generalized world of Persia which serves as a blind for his satire on France. As his ideal observer, Usbek first seeks to understand men and their actions in the aggregate, then to generalize about society. This combination of empiricism and deductive rationalism is the method Montesquieu used again in *The Spirit of the Laws*.

In the course of their travels in Europe, Usbek and Rica, who are in search of justice, have occasion to criticize every facet of European life. The pope is seen as a "magician," the church as a vested interest, and bishops as concocters of a faith which they dispense through fraudulent indulgences. Wars are fought for expansion and glory, not, as they should be, to defend the land or to aid allies. Politics is "a science which teaches princes to what lengths they may carry the violation of justice without injuring their own interests." Corruption, poverty, exploitation, and an omnipresent ennui, all receive their due. As for the European view of insanity, Usbek observes, "these Frenchmen . . . shut up a few madmen in a house to convince people that those outside are not mad."

But if Usbek is a positive character in his role as a disinterested traveler and observer, he is negative in his role as master of a Persian harem. The free-floating critic is in conflict with the citizen whose actions accord with the despotic political traditions of his homeland. In concentrating the positive and negative in a single character, Montesquieu intensified the conflict of interests between philosophy, politics, and ethics, and by implication their interdependence. This conflict is most apparent in his handling of the erotic which is the underlying theme of the *Letters.*

Usbek's prolonged absence from the harem causes a crisis. The letters he receives from his wives are filled with despair, and those from his eunuchs with complaints about the difficulty of controlling the situation. The relationship between a master, who is now an absentee lover, and the women, whose love and lust he has aroused and then left in the care of eunuchs, is the condition for revolt in the seraglio. Soon all the women are insubordinate, except his favorite, Roxane. Furious, Usbek orders his eunuchs to restore order at whatever cost. The grand eunuch is murdered, and his successor, Solim, initiates a reign of terror to purify the harem. Finally, after Roxane has repeatedly warned Usbek to return, even she is unfaithful. The last letter, to Usbek from Roxane, who is on the verge of suicide, rises to almost tragic heights:

> How could you have thought that I was naïve enough to imagine that I was put in the world only to adorn your whims? That while you pampered yourself with everything, you should have the right to mortify all my desires? No! I might have lived in servitude, but I have always

been free. I have rewritten your laws after the laws of nature, and my spirit has ever sustained itself in independence.

You should continue to be thankful to me for the sacrifice I have made to you, thankful that I lowered myself to the point of seeming faithful to you, and thankful because I kept in my cowardly heart all that I should have proclaimed to the whole earth. Finally, you should be thankful that I have dared profane the name of virtue by allowing submission to your fancy to be called by that name.

Roxane's suicide is the protest of nature outraged by despotism, the despotism of sex. It is clear from her letter that, according to the "laws of nature," human beings are born to self-fulfillment in freedom, mutuality in love, and virtue in society. True love, which is stifled in the seraglio, epitomizes this humanistic ideal. Conversely, the suppression or disfigurement of nature spells its doom. Reason, therefore, could not consist in "enabling us to transcend the empirical world but rather in teaching us to feel at home in it" (Ernst Cassirer). Its function, for Montesquieu, as for most of the *philosophes,* was to bring about a perfect accord between natural and human law. From this point of view, suicide under despotism could be a rational act. Usbek himself, in condemning the European attitude toward suicide, asks: "Why should I be forced to labor for a society to which I refuse to belong?"—finding himself in the end the unwitting victim of his own reasoning. Lessing and Goethe both appealed to Montesquieu's defense of suicide, precisely on account of its humanistic ethical and revolutionary political implication.

The claims of nature and those of reason were thus closely linked in Montesquieu's mind, the latter being the perfection and fulfillment of the former. The two are not intrinsically at odds; if they are set asunder this is due to an uncongenial political system. The erotic served to dramatize the relationship between the individual and the larger political structure in which he lives out his personal life, the relationship between the most private and the most public realms of life. The great crime of despotism is just that, in suppressing freedom, it also ruins human nature. Not only does it reduce a population to the animal level of slaves, like the inmates of Usbek's harem; the men who carry out his orders are also unnatural, like his eunuchs. So long as the master is present the seraglio can function. In his absence, however, it becomes clear that what enabled him to preserve order when he was present was fear. In *The Spirit of the Laws*, fear becomes the "law" of despotism, and the oriental seraglio its "ideal type."

The Spirit of the Laws

Montesquieu undertook in this vast treatise to seek out those political forms which would or would not enable us to feel at home in the world. Asking how people develop and behave living under different political systems, and what kinds of men these various systems encourage, suppress, and corrupt, he became the first modern thinker to attempt to create a science of society. However, unlike his nineteenth- and twentieth-century successors in sociology, Auguste Comte and Emile Durkheim, Montesquieu would have distrusted a science which views society in terms of the same laws as those governing the physical world. He would have disputed Durkheim's claim "that the laws of society are no different from those governing the rest of nature and that the method by which they are discovered

is identical with that of the other sciences." On the contrary, he turned to nature precisely in order to explain
those political and social phenomena, like despotism, which
are not intelligible from the standpoint of reason and
morality. On Montesquieu's view, any method of social
study which fails to distinguish between its "laws of society" and "those governing the rest of nature," rather than
explaining social breakdown would be symptomatic of
breakdown. And any social science which asserted that the
methods by which the laws of society are discovered "is
identical with that of the other sciences" would be tantamount to giving tacit support to the forces conducing to
the degradation of society.

A true science of the human world and the art of
politics were inseparable in his mind. Like all of the enlighteners, Montesquieu felt keenly that knowledge is and
should be a factor in shaping society; or, as Ernst Cassirer
states it, that thought "consists not only in analyzing and
dissecting, but in actually bringing about the order of things
which it conceives as necessary, so that by this act of fulfillment it may demonstrate its reality and truth." When he
wrote, "The intelligent world is far from being so well
governed as the physical," he did not mean that the intelligent world *should* be governed by the physical, but only
that what prevents it from being so well governed is the
nature of men "which requires them to be free agents."
The fact that men have never been content to conform, like
nature, to any set of particular laws, not even "those of
their own instituting," convinced Montesquieu that the
"spirit" in which laws are adopted, modified, and eventually
abandoned must be the essence of human nature. If he
expanded his study of political and social structures far
beyond despotism, he did so in the belief that, throughout

history, no system of laws has ever fully allowed men to develop their nature; the misery of oppression has always been made to seem more attractive than freedom.

It was to the "spirit" of the laws, therefore, rather than in the laws themselves, that Montesquieu looked for the living expression of man's true nature. To what extent, he asked, is the action of a lawgiver in accordance with the normal (free) nature of men, and what explains deviations from this norm? In order to answer these questions it was necessary to know *how* societies evolve, not just *that* they do. It was necessary to recognize the element of continuity in a particular society in order to recognize what constitutes change. In seeking to describe and explain social types historically, he distinguished between "the nature and principle of government, the former being that by which it is constituted, the latter that by which it is made to act. One is its particular structure, and the other the human passions which set it in motion" (Bk. III, chap. 1). In tracing the variety of laws and institutions back to their "nature and principle," he discovered three basic types of political structure: despotism founded on fear, monarchy on honor, and republics on virtue. He did not say that each of these necessarily *should* persist. On the contrary, he condemned despotism and favored a constitutional monarchy; that is, a *mixture* of the monarchical and republican forms. He did say, however, that these are the three basic types of government which have in fact evolved in the course of history, and that *if* they are to maintain themselves according to their nature, each requires just *its* principle and no other. "Such are the principles of the three governments: which does not signify that in a certain republic one is virtuous, but that one ought to be so. This does not prove that in a certain monarchy one has a sense of honor, and that in a particular despotic state one has a sense of fear, but that one ought to have such: *without these qualities the government will be imperfect* (Bk. III, chap. 11).

When Montesquieu declared that "Laws, in their most general signification, are the necessary relations arising from the nature of things" (Bk. I, chap. 1), he had in mind therefore two interlocking relations. One was the *logical* relationship between the "nature and principle of government" which, if it really obtained, would be the sign of a perfect (*i.e.* coherent, intelligible, self-consistent) system. The other was their *actual* relationship. He drew this distinction because he found that the two are rarely completely consistent with each other. On the other hand, he sought always to arrive at the logical only by inference from the actual. He used the word law in both senses, having observed that what is rational is what most often exists in reality, even if only in a potential, distorted, or partially realized form. "There is . . . a prime reason, and laws are the relations subsisting between it and different things, and the relations of these to one another" (Bk. I, chap. 1). On Montesquieu's view, the logical and actual relationships between the "nature and principle of government" interact and determine the basic structure of the state. This method, which was grounded in empirical reality without being altogether subject to it, he used to evaluate the (functional) perfection of the various political systems at any given stage of their development. So long as the principle of government remains rationally consistent with its nature, the government can survive, even if burdened by bad laws. "When once the principles of government are corrupted, the very best laws become bad and turn against the state; when the principles are sound, even bad laws have the effect of good ones. The force of the principle carries everything with it" (Bk. VIII, chap. 11). Should its principle deteriorate, however, the state is doomed, no matter how good its laws. "The corruption of every government begins almost always with the corruption of its principles" (Bk. VIII, chap. 1). This corrosion of principles Montesquieu traced to the peculiar susceptibilities of each form of government to the action of the various natural and social forces which act on society.

Durkheim later took the position that "a discipline which looks to the future lacks a determinate subject matter and should therefore be called not a science but an art." At the same time, he voiced the common objection that Montesquieu failed to see that "every society embodies conflicting factors, simply because it has gradually emerged from a past form and is tending toward a future one. He failed to recognize a process, whereby a society, while remaining faithful to its nature, is constantly becoming something new." The fact is that no one knew better than Montesquieu that "every society embodies conflicting factors," which is exactly why the goal of his political philosophy was the restoration of an equilibrium, the resolution of contending forces. And if his study "looks to the future," which supposedly disqualifies it as a science, it is because he did recognize that every society is indeed "tending toward a future form." The presupposition of his writing on the rise and fall of the Romans, as well as that of *The Laws*, is precisely that mankind, through a proper understanding of the totality of forces that shape society, can break out of the tragic cycle of growth and decline.

Montesquieu has also been criticized, on the one hand, for having overestimated the role of the lawmaker in the complex of factors at work in society, and, on the other, for having regarded laws merely as a reflection of the milieu in which they originate. He saw no contradiction, however, in admitting that the lawmaker operates within a system of forces, yet interprets and activates them, sets them in motion in a particular direction. A people becomes subject to the forces of nature or tradition only if its legislators are ignorant of them or unwilling to counteract them. For example, bad legislators will submit to the immoral influences of climate, while good legislators are those who establish laws which will arouse the moral energies of society to resist them (Bk. XIV, chap. 5). By recognizing the forces at work, the wise legislator can guide them toward a goal of his own choosing.

The inadequacy of Montesquieu's concrete system of classification, and the defectiveness and obsolescence of much of the empirical data he used to support it, have long been recognized. But these shortcomings do not necessarily vitiate the fundamentals of his system which is not concerned solely with empirical data, but also with their rational relationship. Nor do they vitiate the search for knowledge intended to enable the legislator, who, Montesquieu believed, is responsible in the last analysis for what forces will act determinately in shaping society, to recognize and fulfill his task: that of bringing about a harmonious equilibrium between the "physical" and "intelligent" worlds in such a way as to enhance human liberty. Freedom, for Montesquieu, was moral freedom, consisting "only in the power of doing what we ought to will, and in not being constrained to do what we ought not to will" (Bk. XI, chap. 3). He believed that freedom in this sense was realizable only under a government based on the separation of powers, where laws are enacted by an elected legislature, administered by a separate executive, and enforced by an independent judiciary. For only under such a government is no man "compelled to do things to which the law does not oblige him, nor forced to abstain from things which the law permits" (Bk. XI, chap. 4). The free human being envisaged by Montesquieu was one who is moral yet at home in the world, moral *because* he is at home in the world.

Montesquieu's failings lay less in his approach to the study of society than in his political conservatism. In method, he was the forerunner of the radicals Rousseau and Marx as well as of the conservatives Burke and Savigny. It was his political views which caused his younger contemporaries to be cool toward him. "As to our aristocrats and petty despots of all grades," Helvétius wrote to him, "if they understand you, they cannot praise you too much, and this is the fault I have ever found with the principles of your work. . . ." His conservatism limited his outlook to the extent that he never really believed in the eventual realization of his own ideal, never really believed that the "physical" and the "intelligent" worlds could ever be reconciled, nor that a society would or could conform to its own laws "so exactly as the physical world." His doctrine of the separation of powers and his political ideal of a mixed government, which were modelled on the Newtonian view of the static equilibrium of forces in the universe, were conceived less as instruments of progress than as safeguards against a relapse into despotism. Yet, in seeking to define the political structure which could reconcile the claims of nature and those of freedom, Montesquieu made the great discovery of the interconnection between political patterns and the totality of forces, both natural and social, which act on society. He discovered that laws and institutions form a superstructure built upon and interacting with tradition, custom, and economic and physical factors. These discoveries paved the way for the study of comparative politics, comparative law, and the social sciences.

Prévost and the Problem of Love

While Montesquieu was at work on *The Spirit of the Laws,* the theme of the antagonism between man's physical and moral nature, and the role of reason in reestablishing their unity, was taken up again by Antoine-François Prévost (1697–1763) in his *Manon Lescaut* (1731), one of the few great French novels of the century and one of the masterpieces of literature on love. Although Montesquieu himself approved of this writing, because "love is a noble motive," Prévost's purpose was not to eulogize erotic love. On the contrary, as a Christian moralist he was concerned to show that passion is man's greatest enemy, that it stands in diametrical opposition to virtue and true happiness. He saw love as something "violent, unjust, cruel; capable of any excess and yielding to it without remorse. Deliver us from love!" he pleaded. Prévost admired Richardson's *Pamela,* which he translated in 1742 and helped popularize in Europe, because it was "completely purged of all imagery which, in too many writings, composed for simple amusement, tend to inflame the heart rather than instruct it." However, instead of appealing to the saving power of Christian faith in his campaign against passion, he invoked the new ideas of his age, reason and deism. If salvation were possible at all, and Prévost was doubtful, it could be attained only through the use of reason. Both he and Montesquieu, though from quite different points of view, evaluated reason positively, not as an end in itself, but as a means to the end of a fully realized life.

A Benedictine monk, a soldier, wanderer, editor of an important literary journal, then a monk again, this "Ishmael of literature," as F. C. Greene called him, was never secure in his religious faith. He entered the cloister in the first place in search of a refuge against "the weakness of his heart." Unhappy in monastic confinement, he left his abbey in 1728 without permission and spent six years in exile in England and Holland, where he devoted himself to a six volume romance entitled *Memoires of a Man of Quality*. He reentered religious life in 1734, having received papal permission to transfer to a freer congregation. Nowhere do we sense more clearly the profound change that the age was undergoing than in his attempt to reconcile two mutually antagonistic outlooks, in his sensitive effort to shore up traditional Christian values by appeal to new philosophical ideas. While rejecting Montesquieu's humanistic ideal, Prévost unwittingly strengthened its appeal. Although he wished to alert the human heart against the danger of passion, his depiction of erotic love was so compelling and sincere that it had the very opposite effect from what he intended. It is in this capacity that *Manon* gave expression to and exercised a formative influence on the emerging Enlightenment.

The hero of the novel is the studious and chaste young Chevalier des Grieux who meets and falls in love with the beautiful commoner, Manon. They run off and try to live together on the little money he has with him. For a time they are happy. But Manon, though she loves him, is addicted to luxury and pleasure, and she secretly becomes the mistress of a wealthy financier. Though this means of raising money is of little concern to her, since her heart is still with des Grieux, he considers this betrayal apostasy. After being returned home forcibly, he resumes his studies and seems well on the way to recovery as a seminary student. But one day Manon turns up, professes her love for him, and he abandons family, friends, and ecclesiastical career to be with her. Thereafter, his decline is rapid. Manon deceives him repeatedly, only to return and win him back again. In order to keep her he becomes a card sharp, a cheat, and finally a murderer. In the end she is arrested and deported to America as a prostitute. Des Grieux follows her, only to see their prospects for happiness ruined anew and his lover die. He buries her and returns to France resolved "to atone, by a wise and orderly life" for his scandalous conduct.

Lucid and simple in style, compelling in the naïveté of its sentiments, the unhappy story of this illicit love captured the popular imagination and won Manon and her chevalier a lasting place in literature and music. Although Prévost had no reason to think he had written a dangerous book, it was banned in 1733, the same year which saw the first publication of Voltaire's *Letters on the English*. According to the distinguished literary historian, Erich Auerbach, *Manon Lescaut* represents an intermediary phase between the seventeenth-century taste for the sublime and the tragic and the hard realism of the high Enlightenment which stressed the natural, the material, and the useful. The theme of the sublime, which became lachrymose in Prévost, began to lose in tragic seriousness right from the beginning of the century, although the age continued to favor the graceful, the witty, and the elegant. This development was due to the new tendency to fuse "the sentimental and the ethical, the realistic and the serious" (Auerbach);

a tendency which led to full-blown Romanticism, on the one hand, and to the rational realism of the encyclopedists on the other. In contrast to the practice of seventeenth-century classicism of keeping the two realms sharply separated, there now occurs, in Prévost and Voltaire both, a mixture of styles which is the product of the "increasingly bourgeois cast of society." The characters in eighteenth-century literature, as Auerbach shows, are no longer detached from the material conditions of their existence; they are "embedded in circumstances . . . on which they are dependent, and in which they are enmeshed materially and even spiritually."

Manon Lescaut, therefore, does not mark merely a change in style. Rather this change itself was rooted in the changed conditions of society and in Prévost's view of life and morality as it was formed under the influence of the "increasingly bourgeois cast of society." In the introduction to the novel he refers to his hero as "an ambiguous character, a mixture of virtues and vices, a perpetual contrast of good sentiments and bad actions." He attributes "this contradiction between our ideas and our conduct" to the fact that, "since all moral precepts are only vague, general principles, it is very hard to apply them specifically in detail to our behavior and actions." In seventeenth-century France, where the social structure was more stable and class lines more clearly drawn, and where men generally recognized and accepted their place in society, like the ideal honnête homme, moral precepts were not regarded as "vague, general principles," but rather as clear and universal imperatives. The problem of right conduct lay precisely in the fact that these moral precepts were absolute and allowed for no compromise, deviation, or flexibility in their application. For Prévost, living at a time when such sta-

bility was crumbling and the social structure was undergoing profound changes, experience was all that could
serve as a reliable guide to proper conduct. Moreover, even
experience "is not an advantage that everyone is free to
gain; it depends on the different situations in which we
find ourselves placed by fortune. So there remains only
example that can serve for many people as a rule in the
practice of virtue." *Manon*, therefore, was intended to serve
as ersatz experience and as a vehicle for moral enlightenment. "Each deed that is here reported is a degree of
enlightenment, an instruction that substitutes for experience; each adventure is a model on which to form oneself;
all it needs is to be adjusted to the circumstances one is in.
The entire work is a treatise on morality shown entertain-
ingly in practice."

Prévost's mixing of styles, then, was an artistic requirement imposed on him by the social realities he confronted and the characteristic moral problems they posed.
He wished to save the sublime but found that in order to
do so, he was forced to immerse it in the real. So, on the
one hand, he portrayed his lovers as basically good, despite
their shameful actions. Even Manon is not evil, only corrupted. On the other hand, *Manon* is neither a novel of
social criticism nor one of philosophical propaganda: "The
social milieu is an established frame of reference, which is
accepted as it happens to be." (Auerbach) Whereas *The
Persian Letters* shows a far better grasp of the problem of
society but falls somewhat short as a work of art, *Manon*
is a successful artistic creation which is all the more realistic in that it faithfully but disinterestedly reflects society.
In a tearful love story, whose "effectiveness in the border
region between the soul and the senses is exploited and
found to be especially suited to produce the then fashion-

able thrill of mingled sentiment and eroticism" (Auerbach), the fact that the heroine is of "common birth" is bound to be significant, when it is a question of a love relationship between her and a chevalier in a society still sharply divided into classes. If Manon is not innately wicked, if she is "embedded in circumstances" on which she is dependent, and in which she is "enmeshed materially and even spiritually," then her vulgar conception of the good life must be traceable to them. It was, after all, the goal of aspiring bourgeois, which she saw all around her, to gain access to and simulate the life of the ne'er-do-well nobility. Precisely because Prévost accepts the social milieu "as it happens to be," all the more telling is it that his des Grieux extols America to Manon as a place where one no longer need reckon with the "arbitrary laws of rank and convention."

Nor, as a realist, does Prévost fail to establish that money, or rather the lack of it, is the chief source of his lovers' difficulties. Usually high-flown, and often guilty of "cloudy, contour-blurring, overemotional rhetoric," (Auerbach) Prévost has his chevalier reflect at one point: "Love is stronger than plenty, stronger than treasures and riches, but it needs their help; and nothing makes a lover more desperate than to see himself dragged down by that, in spite of himself, to the coarseness of the basest souls." And nowhere is the fusion of the sentimental and the ethical, the realistic and the serious, more evident that in des Grieux's humanistic defense of love against the Christian conception of virtue—a defense which Prévost himself rejected, but more because lasting love was unrealizable, in his eyes, than because it was intrinsically invalid.

> Will you say, as the mystics do, that what torments the body is happiness to the soul? You will not dare say so;

it is an indefensible paradox. So this happiness that you exalt so highly is mingled with a thousand sufferings, or, to speak more accurately, is nothing but a web of unhappinesses through which one strives toward felicity. Now if the power of the imagination makes men find pleasure in these very ills, because they may lead to a happy goal for which we hope, why do you label as contradictory and senseless, in my conduct, a completely similar disposition? . . . The only conclusion I want to reach here is that there is no worse way to turn a heart away from love than to decry its delights and promise more happiness in the exercise of virtue. From the way we are made, it is certain that our felicity consists in pleasure: I defy anyone to form another idea of it; now the heart has no need of long consultation with itself to feel that of all pleasures the sweetest are those of love.

Virtue, for Prévost, is still on the side of religion, and reason and passion are incompatible because the rational man pursues virtue. Des Grieux concedes that "the goal of virtue is infinitely superior to that of love." But, if he could not envisage the reconciliation of reason and passion, he at least regrets their opposition, as we see in des Grieux's lamentation: "Alas! Yes, it is my duty to act according as I reason! But is action within my power? What aid would I not need in order to forget Manon's charms?" Like Montesquieu, Prévost was transitional between two worlds, the Old Regime and the now assertive bourgeois world-view. Both were able to grasp the human dilemma involved in this transition, but neither was able to provide a progressive solution to it. On the one hand, they both deplored the conflict between natural and moral man. On the other, neither fully ascribed to reason the power to remedy it, with the result that their distinction between good and evil is no longer clear-cut. Montesquieu tended toward a cautious relativism and Prévost toward outright despair. For both, the problem of right conduct was one of adapting to circumstances which were in some respects evil and in other respects relatively good. To have attributed to reason alone the power to effect the humanistic unity of being would have implied, as the later enlighteners realized, a thoroughgoing transformation of the social and political environment. The further evolution of the Enlightenment required the ascription of this power to reason and hence its transformation into a weapon against the Old Regime. This would be the work of François Arouet (1694–1778), who took the more dashing pen-name, Voltaire, and proceeded to make himself the greatest publicist and foremost fighter on behalf of reason that the world has ever seen.

Voltaire and Natural Religion

The noted French scholar, Gustav Lanson, has called the *Letters on the English* "the first bomb hurled against the Old Regime." Voltaire, of course, was not the first to criticize French society. But his *Letters,* based on his exile in England (1726–1729), was the first writing which sought to free reason from any association with the institutions and values of the Old Regime and turn it against them. The chain of events which led up to this work began with an exchange of insults between this bold young wit and the chevalier de Rohan. For his impudence Voltaire was beaten by the chevalier's lackeys, imprisoned in the Bastille, and released only on condition that he go immediately into exile in England. There he enjoyed the company of Pope, Swift, and Gay, and discovered the writings of Bacon,

Locke, and Newton. When he returned to France he was no longer merely the clever *enfant terrible* whose lampoons against the Regent had gotten him into trouble earlier; his quick and brilliant mind, his strong sense of individuality, his scepticism and deism were now steeped in English empiricism and freethinking. He now devoted himself to the prodigious task of enlightening France and eventually all of mankind. Using his pen as a weapon to this end, he proceeded to pour out plays, poems, pamphlets, histories, novels, treatises, and translations which add up to seventy some volumes. According to Lanson's figures, thirty-four complete editions of his works, and many incomplete ones, were published between 1778 and 1835. During one seven-year period a million and a half copies of his books were sold. If he did not succeed in his self-assigned task, he did at least make himself the best known and the most feared and respected writer of the century.

If Voltaire does not impress us today as much as he did his own generation, this is partly because the causes for which he fought have in the main been won: his battle against the church, feudal privilege, and religious intoler-ance; his struggle for personal liberty, legal equality, and freedom of thought and expression. This legacy is so natural to a healthy liberal society that it is usually taken for granted. If, for all of his writing, Voltaire made no original contribution to philosophy or science, and if his literary and historical works are, with a few exceptions, scarcely read today, we must remember that his aim after 1729 was to bring about a new order of things. It was to this end that he devoted his powerful mind, vast knowledge, and brilliant pen. All the enlighteners viewed France as unnatural and looked to reason as the means to discover the just and ideal order of society as prescribed by nature. All of them regarded nature as the embodiment of "all truths which are capable of a purely immanent justification, and which require no transcendent revelation but are certain in themselves" (Cassirer). But it was Voltaire, more than any other single *philosophe,* who forged these views into an ideology, the ideology of the bourgeoisie.

In his *Letters* he praises England as the land of liberty, tolerance, and common sense, using it, like Montesquieu, though with different motives, as a stick with which to beat France. (America would serve the same purpose after 1770). He extols Bacon as the herald of modern science, Newton for having demonstrated that the universe is infinite and uniform throughout, governed by "purely immanent" laws, and Locke for having shown that men are rational beings for whom knowledge is the means to achieve earthly happiness. He especially applauds Locke as the man who successfully refuted the Cartesian doctrine of innate ideas and reconstructed philosophy on the Aristotelian view that "all our ideas originate in the senses." The combination of Newton's science and Locke's philosophy suggested to him that scepticism could be curbed and channeled into a positive approach to society, religion, and ethics. For if men are shaped by an infinite nature which functions in accordance with universal and rational laws, then they are capable of bringing their thoughts, actions, and institutions into harmony with it. Voltaire drew the conclusion that, while God has a place in this system, His function is limited to the creation of it and of a human race capable of comprehending its workings. God, for him, was like a "constitutional monarch who, having made laws, Himself agreed to abide by them" (Martin). Nature, having absorbed God's attributes, could now claim to be the only basis for religion. Under the impact of this claim, orthodox Christianity began to give way to the *natural* religion of deism. "I understand by natural religion," Voltaire writes, "the principle of morality common to the whole human race." The rational orderliness of Newton's universe implied a creator, as a watch implies a watchmaker. Accordingly, deism retained the belief in a divine being as a first principle. But there was no place in it for revelation, original sin, or grace, without which orthodoxy cannot stand. Deism was the spiritual weapon used by the enlighteners to oppose orthodoxy and already pointed in the direction of atheism.

Voltaire, who was in the forefront of this struggle against orthodox Christianity, singled out Pascal as the chief obstacle to the triumph of deism. The most profound modern apologist for the orthodox position, Pascal had challenged reason to find a doctrine better suited than Christianity to explain the evil and discord in the world, and man's apparently contradictory nature. In his view, man was both divine and animal by nature. The ambivalence of human nature, the futility of human aspirations to perfection, man's sense of being tossed between "the infinite and nothingness"—these, Pascal believed, could be explained satisfactorily only by the doctrine of original sin, against which reason is powerless. "What will become of you, O man, who try by your reason to discover what is your true condition? . . . Know then, proud creature, what a paradox you are to yourself. Be humble, impotent reason; be quiet, imbecile nature; learn from your Master of our true condition, of which you are ignorant. Hearken unto God!"

Against this "sublime misanthrope," Voltaire maintained that belief in God is feasible only as an inference from the observable realm of nature where alone God is manifest to man. It is an act of reason, not of faith. Voltaire rejected not only the pessimistic theology of Pascal, however, but also the optimistic metaphysics of Leibniz and Pope who conceived the universe as a preestablished harmony in which "whatever is, is right" (Pope). In Voltaire's view, this philosophy does not save man from the depressing Christian doctrine of total depravity; such optimism he calls rather "desperation—a cruel philosophy under a soothing name." "My dear Pope," he wrote, "my poor hunchback, who told you that God could not have formed you without a hump?" And was not the Lisbon earthquake of 1755 a sufficient refutation of such "worthless bliss"? To deny the reality of evil was simply to add one more evil to all those that already existed. Voltaire thus ended up rejecting both pessimism and optimism. In doing so, however, he confronted the problem of providing a new explanation for the existence of evil.

Hume and the Problem of God

According to deism, nature is the work of God and man the product of nature. Man and all that he thinks and does are therefore in harmony with the laws of nature and thus in harmony with God. This means that evil logically can be conceived only as unnatural behavior. But if everything accords with the laws of nature, how is evil possible? How could deism possibly answer Pascal's question: "Why is custom not natural?" Without intending it, Voltaire brought to a head the "ugly dilemma" of the new philosophy: "if nature is good, then there is no evil in the world; if there is evil in the world, then nature is so far not good" (Becker).

It was David Hume (1711–1776), addressing himself to the problem of theodicy, who first exposed the philosophical dilemma of deism. In his *Inquiry Concerning Human Understanding*, he takes the position that no religious hypothesis satisfactorily explains the existence of evil in the world. "We never can have reason to infer any attributes or any principles of action in him [i.e., in the divinity], but so far as we have known them to have been exerted and satisfied." According to Hume, the inference of a just God from nature was an ill-conceived attempt on the part of deism to transform traditional Christianity into a rational doctrine.

> While we argue from the course of nature and infer a particular intelligent cause which first bestowed and still preserves order in the universe, we embrace a principle which is still uncertain and useless. It is uncertain because the subject lies entirely beyond the reach of human experience. It is useless because our knowledge of this cause being derived entirely from the course of nature, we can never, according to the rules of just reasoning, return back from the cause with any new inference or, making additions to the common and experienced course of nature, establish any principles of conduct and behavior.

The deist inference of a just God from nature, according to Hume, was a "mere *possibility* and hypothesis," but not a necessary cause and effect relationship which can be known as something objective and universally valid. His attack on deism originated in his critique of causality in general. In his *Inquiry*, he maintains that the concept of cause is indeed the indispensable foundation of all knowledge, but since causality cannot be demonstrated, the validity of knowledge itself is questionable. Experience only shows the succession of events but does not reveal any intrinsic necessity in the relation of their succession. It is habit or custom that induces us involuntarily to expect that one event will invariablly follow from another. But habit and custom are not knowledge: neither justifies us in concluding from the past to the future. Causality is a product of our thinking, not a principle which necessarily corresponds to the real order of things. "It is itself merely a product of the play of ideas which are connected by no objective, rational principles, but in their combination simply follow the workings of the imagination and obey its mechanical laws" (Cassirer).

Hume's views reflected and gave direction to a change taking place around mid-century in science itself. The question arose as to whether science had not simply substituted for religion a new materialistic metaphysics. Was the rational structure of the universe really demonstrable, really given in experience? Or was it not rather a presupposition of experience? And, if the latter, was not this presupposition just as arbitrary as any philosophical or theological premise? Hume concluded that the uniformity of nature is an axiom, not a proof of the validity of scientific statements. Science is justified in subscribing to this axiom on the grounds of practical necessity. The possibility of purposeful action requires the assumption that what we learn from past and present experience will be valid with regard to the future. To reject this assumption would mean the negation of man's whole empirical and social existence. In other words, the rational order of nature is only a premise; a useful one, one necessary to action, but a premise nonetheless. In this respect science is similar to religion. Neither is capable of strictly rational and objective truths; both are grounded, as Hume tried to show, in the subjective realm of psychological necessity. Even matter cannot be said to be anything more than the sum of observable qualities by which it is known.

But if the premises on which science was founded were just as tenuous as philosophical or religious premises, science still could claim a crucial advantage over these other forms of thought in that it recognized its premises as such and accorded to them no more than a hypothetical status. Science thus reduced metaphysics to method. In denying to the physical universe any transcendent qualities, in purging itself of all transcendent assumptions, science succeeded in ridding itself of the main obstacles to progress in man's understanding of the empirical world. At the same time, Hume's scepticism seemed to result in what later in the century Kant would call a "philosophical scandal": reality seemed to dissolve into appearance and knowledge into mere opinion. There occurred a gradual shift in emphasis from the mathematical sciences to experimentation and the sciences dealing with the origin and evolution of the physical order—a shift which stemmed as much from *doubt about* the existence of an objectively real and rationally necessary universe as it did from *confidence in* the existence of such a universe. Corresponding to this shift in emphasis, philosophy gradually turned from seeking to know about things to understanding the thought process itself. The harvest of scepticism was the growing conviction that the only certainty we can attain to is the certainty of the mind and the laws according to which it functions.

If Hume drew a sharp distinction between fact and value, between the *is* and the *ought*, it was not to depreciate the *ought*, but rather to prevent the specious derivation of value from fact. If he limited reason solely to the function of determining facts, it was not to deny the importance of

values, but only to show that man is more than his reason;
that reason is but one tool in guiding him in his search for
values. Hume ironically commented that "any person
seasoned with a just sense of the imperfections of natural
reason will fly to revealed truth with the greatest avidity."
But this was not the only conclusion to be drawn from his
doctrine, as Rousseau and Kant would show. Scepticism
had the salutary effect of undermining the view that nature
acts on man in a mechanistic cause and effect manner. It
thus opened a way out of the impasse into which deism had
brought ethics.

Voltaire's *Candide*: the Ethics of Enlightenment

The dilemma was not immediately bypassed, however. Voltaire, in coming to grips with the problem of evil,
dramatized this philosophical reorientation. Inadvertently,
he confirmed the very position he wished to discredit;
namely Pascal's view that reason alone, since it can never
discover man's "true condition," must end in scepticism.
Having rejected both pessimism and optimism, and never
willing to abandon deism for fear that the world would seem
altogether arbitrary and meaningless, Voltaire found himself, as he grew older, succumbing to scepticism. No doubt
his personal experiences partly contributed to this end. At
the end of the forties, a happy and productive period for him,
there was the infidelity and untimely death of his remarkable mistress, the Marquise du Châtelet. There was
his disillusionment with Frederick the Great as a philos-
opher-king, during the years he spent at the Prussian court
in the early fifties. Then there was the bitter sense of man's
helplessness he felt with regard to the Lisbon earthquake.

These experiences, in combination with his growing sense of the indifference of the universe toward man's fate, put him to the test. His state of mind, the state of mind of the age at this point, found supreme expression in *Candide* (1759). In this most living of all his writings, Voltaire seems to be saying that we can neither avoid evil nor eradicate it; whatever happiness man may know lies in his recognition and denunciation of evil without hope of overcoming it. Voltaire comes full circle in this philosophical novel, arriving at a position similar to that of Pascal. From a social standpoint, he found himself, like his archenemy, caught between an ideological affinity with the middle class, on the one hand, and an attachment to a monarchy which was diverging increasingly from the real interest of that class on the other. In dramatizing the moral dilemma of the age in all its amplitude, *Candide* marks a major turning-point in European thought; the transition from a spiritualistic to a materialistic moral orientation.

Candide stands between the optimist, Dr. Pangloss (a caricature of Leibniz), who denies the reality of evil, and the pessimist, Martin, who believes that evil is real and inherent in this world which is torn by an eternal struggle between the supernatural forces of good and evil. These attitudes have in common the fact that they are both passive, accepting things as they are. Both justify the existing situation and incline the individual to sink into apathy by denying the prospect of improvement. Voltaire plays them off against each other in the destiny of Candide and his beloved Cunegonde who suffer one misfortune after another in this "best of all possible worlds." Outraged, beaten, robbed, cheated—the victims nonetheless seem comic because their bright expectations contrast so vividly with their dreadful misfortunes. Pessimism and optimism cancel each other in the crucible of reality, and Voltaire achieves his comic effect by juxtaposing empirical truth to metaphysical fiction in a series of incidents that progress in almost slapstick fashion. The tale ends with only a tentative resolution of the ethical dilemma: The problem of evil is regarded as insoluble, speculation as vain, and action and thought as mutually exclusive. "Let us work without theorizing; 'tis the only way to make life endurable."

The world of Candide is one of misery and injustice; the happy man, such as he is, is one who quietly "cultivates his garden." Getting involved in the world only invites trouble, so the wise man stays at home and minds his own business. Nature replaces providence in *Candide,* but in such a way as to eclipse the human condition which is depicted simply as a by-product of nature. Reason enables the wise man to realize only that action results in anguish and abstention from action in ennui. Candide's policy combines two negative recommendations: to remain aloof from the world so as to avoid suffering, and to labor in order not to think. "Work," says the wise Turk whom Candide consults, "keeps at bay three great evils: boredom, vice and need." Always a loser when he attempts to act, Candide withdraws from the world to enjoy the only happiness possible in it: a condition of bare, pristine, self-sufficiency reminiscent of the Garden of Eden. The polarization of nature and humanity, ideal and reality, thought and feeling comes to a head in *Candide.*

While Voltaire showed signs of despair in the face of the absurdity of the world, he nonetheless denounced any doctrine which sought to conceal or justify it. As he became increasingly sceptical about the power of reason alone to bring about happiness, he also recognized that, without it, happiness is surely impossible: that the good life on earth

requires the activation of the whole man, man in his capacity to act as well as to reason. And, although he grew
sceptical about the prospect of happiness in general, he
never denied its importance to the good life on earth.
Finally, if he tended to regard the problem of evil as insoluble, he also faced it squarely as one involving man's
relation to the world at large, where alone man works out
his destiny. Some years before his death, Voltaire ironically
summed up his position thus:

> I shall die with the three theological virtues which are
> my consolation: the faith which I have in human reason
> which is beginning to develop in the world; the hope
> that ministers in their boldness and their wisdom will at
> length destroy customs which are as ridiculous as they
> are dangerous; the charity which makes me grieve for
> my neighbor, complain of his bonds, and long for his
> deliverance. So with faith, hope and charity, I end my
> life a good Christian. (Letter of February 13, 1768 to
> the Comte de Leninhaupt.)

HIGH
ENLIGHTENMENT

The Encyclopedia

Not satisfied with Voltaire's vacillating scepticism, the encyclopedists and physiocrats continued to hold to nature as the norm for morality, arriving at a new metaphysics—the metaphysics of materialism. The *Encyclopedia* (1751–1772), the most prodigious intellectual undertaking of the century, was the main vehicle of this development. It provided a public forum for the *philosophes* and greatly helped to consolidate them into a movement; at one time or another during the twenty years of its production almost every leading thinker in France was involved in it. How the editor, Denis Diderot (1713–1784), brought it to completion in the face of Jesuit opposition, official censorship, obstructions in publication and distribution, and discord and defection in the ranks of the contributors, is a saga in itself. Suffice it to say here that the purpose of the *Encyclopedia* was threefold: to serve as a reference work providing information about the crafts and sciences, to serve as a means of education and instruction in every area of learning and practical activity, and to be a clearinghouse for new ideas on religion, politics, and society. The *Encyclopedia* purported not only to give expression to public opinion but also to help shape it—"to change the common way of thinking" (Diderot). Its leading themes were the autonomy of man, the secularization of knowledge and thought, the natural goodness and perfectibility of human nature, and belief in reason and experience, science and progress: in a word, the credo of the Enlightenment. The very idea of a great compendium of knowledge, involving scores of contributors and intended for the education of society at large, presupposed a progressive, secular, and optimistic outlook. The *Encyclopedia* was inspired by the conception of knowledge as a social function, dependent on and aiming at a sound social structure. It was perhaps the finest expression of the utilitarian spirit. In Diderot's words:

> The aim of an encyclopedia is to assemble the knowledge scattered over the face of the earth, to expound its general system to the men with whom we live, and transmit it to the men who will come after us; in order that the labors of past centuries will not have been in vain for the centuries to come; that our children, better instructed than we, may at the same time become more virtuous and happy, and that we may not die without having deserved well of mankind. (Diderot's article, "Encyclopedia.")

The *Encyclopedia* was decidedly more materialistic and empirical in orientation than the outlook of Voltaire. The founders of eighteenth-century materialism took their point of departure from the biological rather than from the mathematical sciences: Julien La Mettrie (1709–1751) from medicine, Holbach (1723–1789) from chemistry, and Diderot from physiology. Whereas Descartes had proceeded from "clear and distinct" *ideas*, the triumph of empiricism and scepticism since Locke had led scientific inquiry to begin with clear and distinct *sensations*. Locke, in his successful attack on the doctrine of innate ideas, had reasserted the view that nothing is in the mind which is not first in the senses. Hume had declared that the observable effects of nature are all that can be known with certainty. Once science began to set aside any idea of transcendence, whether conceived as providence, causality, or substance, the study of nature reduced to the study of nature by means of exact observation.

La Mettrie's Materialism

La Mettrie, in his two most important writings, *The Natural History of the Soul* (1745) and *Man a Machine* (1748), was the first to apply this approach systematically to the study of man himself. He appealed to materialism on the grounds that everything we see around us is nothing but matter under ever-changing forms. On the basis of his medical studies, he concluded that the difference between man and the lower animals is strictly quantitative. If consciousness is found on the higher levels of the ascending scale of being, it cannot be altogether absent on the lower levels, since all life manifests the same basic characteristics. Man occupies the highest place in the hierarchy of being because his physical structure, functions, and needs are the most complex. "Beings without needs," he writes, "are also without mind"—an idea that already foreshadows the theory of evolution. The gratification of physical needs, which is equivalent to happiness, is the driving force of all life. "Nature created us all solely to be happy—yes, all, from the crawling worm to the eagle that soars out of sight in the clouds." Since man is only a part of nature, since he exists only in nature, all aspects of human life including men's moral and intellectual functions are reducible to extension, motion, and sensation: that is, to the observable effects of nature. We read in *Man a Machine:*

> All the investigations which the greatest philosophers have conducted *a priori,* that is to say, by attempting in a way to use the wings of the spirit, have been fruitless. Thus it is only *a posteriori,* or by seeking to discover the soul through the organs of the body, so to speak, that we can reach the highest probability concerning man's own nature, even though one cannot discover with certainty what that nature is.

Locke had contended that all our ideas are entirely dependent on experience. He always maintained that sensation and reflection constitute simply two distinct, though equally necessary, sources of mental life. La Mettrie, and also Étienne Condillac (1715–1780), expanded Locke's theory into a full-blown materialistic doctrine of psychology, according to which forces entirely independent of man determine his whole character and destiny. Here we encounter a strictly mechanistic determinism which raises crucial ethical questions revealing the basic epistemological weakness of Enlightenment thought: the lack of unity between theory and practice. If we are not self-determining and if we cannot fully understand the forces that do determine us, how can we ever expect to understand ourselves? If these forces are independent of us, how can we act on them, so as eventually to bring custom into harmony with nature? Conversely, if man is so completely dominated by nature, how is it that discord develops between the realms of nature and custom in the first place? La Mettrie himself conceded that, when it comes to understanding human nature, his strictly behavorial approach, which sought "to discover the soul through the organs of the body," did not yield certainty, but only a high degree of probability. Even granting this, however, if man does not understand and help shape the forces which determine him, how can he know for sure that he is inevitably and forever subject to them?

Two decades before the appearance of La Mettrie's first major work, a little known Italian thinker, Giambattista Vico (1668–1744), had challenged Cartesian philosophy from a different point of view. In his most important writing, *The New Science* (1725), which came to the attention of a few German thinkers only later in the century, he took the position that the proper study of man is not nature, but rather history. Only history yields certain knowledge because we can comprehend only what we ourselves create. La Mettrie himself sounded the limitation of his naturalistic approach when he mused: "Who knows whether the reason for man's existence is not simply the fact that he exists? Perhaps he was thrown by chance on some spot of the earth's surface, nobody knows how or why, but simply that he must live and die, like mushrooms that appear from one day to the next . . ." Since we cannot know "with certainty" what human nature is, Le Mettrie, who was so opposed to the metaphysics of others, professed himself what amounted to a metaphysical solution: "Let us boldly conclude," he recommends in the absence of proof positive, "that man is a machine, and that in the whole universe there is but a single substance with various modifications."

The concept of natural law, formerly thought to be a universal and necessary rational principle, was reduced by the materialists to nothing more than the observable relationships between material objects. Holding an intermediary position between Locke, who had conceived natural law as sustaining the established moral order, and Hume, for whom

natural law had nothing to do with morality, La Mettrie
viewed natural law as being subversive of the moral order
in the name of one which presumably was better. According to La Mettrie, natural law is, if anything, simply a
"feeling which teaches us what we should not do, because
we would not wish it to be done to us." Their main aim in
making such a strong case for nature was to use it as a
weapon against the whole of the existing order—religion,
priests, superstition, philosophy, government, and education. However, if nature really did have a moral lesson to
teach, how was it that society so obstinately refused to learn
it? Either custom was in fact natural, or nature had to relin-
quish its claim to be a universally valid moral norm; in
either case, there were no grounds left for social criticism.

Holbach, Helvetius, and Physiocratic Theory

The conception of man as composed of particles of
matter, determined by eternal, unalterable laws, of which
self-love is the most outstanding, formed the theoretical
basis of the social teaching of mechanistic materialism.
Holbach and Claude Adriene Helvétius (1715–1771) carried
this teaching to its logical conclusion. Their fatalism was
even more rigid than that of La Mettrie. Holbach held that
all phenomena are bound together in a continuous chain
of causation in which there is no room for chance, but also
none for free will. At the same time, he stressed the need
for knowledge and political reform. If the supernatural no-
tions of God, immortality, and freedom, the chief obstacles
to a rational and scientific understanding of the natural
order, could be banished, men would then adapt their lives
to nature's laws. Frederick the Great, after reading Holbach's *System of Nature*, noted:

> After the author has exhausted all evidence to show that men are guided by a fatalistic necessity in all their actions, he had to draw the conclusion that we are only a sort of machine, only marionettes moved by the hand of a blind power. And yet he flies into a passion against priests, governments, and against the whole educational system; he believes indeed that men who exercise these functions are free even while he proves to them that they are slaves. What foolishness and what nonsense! If everything is moved by necessary causes, then all counsel, all instruction, all rewards and punishments are as superfluous as inexplicable; for one might just as well preach to an oak and try to persuade it to turn into an orange tree. (Quoted in Cassirer, p. 71.)

Helvétius also stressed the need for education and political reform for the moral rehabilitation of mankind. In his most important writing, *On the Mind* (1759), he advanced the argument that each individual, in seeking his own good, contributes to the general good. The same argument was used by the physiocrats to oppose the royalist policy of mercantilism and any sort of government intervention in trade. They claimed that purely egoistic creatures, if left to pursue their private interests unimpeded, would serve the general good because natural law implies a natural harmony of interests. This view became the basis of *laissez-faire* economics, the policy of economic freedom first formulated by François Quesnay (1694–1774), in his *Economic Table* (1758), the best known of the physiocratic writings. A policy according to which abundance is possible only if the price of goods, land, and labor is determined freely, "naturally" (i.e., without interference), was obviously in the best interests of the middle class, although it was not the conscious intention of the physiocrats to serve these interests. On the contrary, they looked upon commerce and industry as "sterile" and on agriculture as the sole source of wealth. Commerce was sterile, in their view, because it involved nothing more than the exchange of commodities of equal value. Industry was viewed similarly because it was thought to involve only the transformation of raw materials into products which fetched a price amounting to no more than the cost of production plus workers' wages. Agriculture, on the other hand, yielded a surplus because it created wealth proportionally far greater than the natural resources it expended. The physiocrats concluded, therefore, that agriculture was the true source of national prosperity. Since they regarded the bourgeoisie as economically sterile, though useful in other respects, they recommended that capitalism be applied to agriculture, rather than to commerce and industry, and that the tax burden be shifted to the landowners—a process similar to what actually had happened in England and elsewhere before the onset of the Industrial Revolution. Precisely on account of their economic uselessness, the bourgeois should be allowed to go their own way, so to speak, freed of any economic restraints or responsibilities; however the aristocracy should be reactivated as an economically useful and politically responsible landowning class. In the light of its agrarian bias, it is ironical that in the end the physiocratic doctrine favored the middle class which took the motto and mentality of *laissez-faire* for its own. To make the *de facto* justification of the bourgeoisie *de jure* was only a question of reversing the terms of what the physiocrats thought was profitable and retaining the principle of *laissez-faire*. This would be the work of Adam Smith.

All agreed that the unrestrained pursuit of pleasure, profit, and property was prescribed by natural law, and all wished to see a fundamental harmony of interests prevail.

Helvétius, however, denied that the harmony of interests aimed at was natural. In his view, it must be created artificially by the scientific application of education and legislation to society and by a system of rewards and penalties. "The majority of the people of Europe," he wrties, "honor virtue in theory; this is the effect of their education. They despise it in practice, which is the effect of their governments. . . . No one in any case has concurred in the public good to his own prejudice, so that the only method of forming virtuous citizens is to unite the interests of the individual with those of the public." This was the utilitarian solution later elaborated by Jeremy Bentham. From the point of view of the conclusions they wished to draw, however, it matters little that Helvétius advocated political reform in the name of utility and the physiocrats the same in the name of natural law. Both generalized the fact into the inevitable, and the inevitable into the just.

Mechanism, Egotism, and Fatalism

From a historical point of view, however, it matters a great deal that natural law theories were first buttressed and eventually superseded by utilitarian ethical arguments, once bourgeois interests no longer needed an external sanction. For this process shows how incompatible the claims of nature and those of virtue actually were in eighteenth-century thought. Instinct and morality, egoism and sociability, self-interest and altruism proved not to be complementary at all. This is why the philosophy of self-interest, in opposing the established social order, continued to seek a moral sanction. Since none could be found either in a practical reality or in a law of reason beyond the ego, a metaphysical sanction was found. Bourgeois materialism rescued man from supernatural determinism only to deliver him over to the determinism of nature. The intrinsic fatalism of this philosophy prevented it from achieving what it was intended to achieve: the translation of humanistic theory into practice. For how could a doctrine which regarded men as slaves of their physical nature enable them to change their social environment or themselves? If men were inevitably subject to the conditions of life of a social system which was still semifeudal, how could even a bourgeois social and political order be brought into being?

In its very zeal to improve society, abstract reason (abstract because it was admittedly unable to grasp objective reality) revealed its incapacity to overcome the antithesis between nature and custom inherited from the seventeenth century. Its failure to do so undermined the humanistic side of rationalism, for the social ethic proclaimed by materialism could not be translated into a theory of action. It is true that, in claiming that thought and action depended on social conditions which could and should be changed, they did hold men responsible for their own history. In this respect they came closer than any previous social critics to a genuinely historical view of the human world. Moreover, in taking the side of the middle class against the nobility, they showed an awareness of social conflict as such. However, in attributing the social milieu and social conflict to the exploitation of society by the government, they made it seem as if the reform of government—revolution "from above" rather than from below— would result automatically in the improvement of society. The reality of enlightened absolutism gave the lie to this notion. Rousseau was the first to expose the inability of Enlightenment theory to serve as the basis for a program of sweeping social change.

The high Enlightenment suffered another serious shortcoming: an overriding intellectualism. It derived virtue, right action, almost exclusively from right thinking. This view made virtue dependent on the acquisition of culture. But the more the age preened itself on its learning, the more it had to reckon with the fact that culture was mainly the privilege of the wealthy classes. Was virtue too, then, the property of the wealthy? There was an obvious discrepancy between the utilitarian definition of virtue and its derivation from a culture monopolized by a minority. This descrepancy gave rise to the question, discussed increasingly throughout the century, as to whether civilization (*i.e.*, the arts and sciences and their effects on human character) actually promoted virtue, especially now that it was defined as the "good life on earth instead of the beatific life after death." The more the *philosophes*—Voltaire, Turgot, Helvétius, and Condorcet outstandingly—proclaimed the progress of civilization, the more salient this question became. While defending virtue, they seemed to be giving support to the very social system they opposed in virtue's name. Rousseau, who attached least importance to intellectual cultivation, ridiculed them for making it the condition of virtue. "We have physicists, geometricians, chemists, astronomers, poets, musicians, and painters in plenty; but we no longer have a citizen among us . . ."

Diderot

Not content with the current formulation of materialism, Diderot asked how a doctrine of strict natural necessity could be reconciled with the obvious fact of change. He recognized that a mechanistic theory which regarded nature as static and uniform failed to account for the appearance of new and ever more complex forms of matter and life, and for the process which gives rise to them. In order to explain fully what things are, it would be necessary to explain how they came to be and what forces make for change. Neither mathematical conceptualization nor the analysis and classification of species satisfactorily answered this need, he contended. Following along the lines laid down by La Mettrie and Georges L. L. de Buffon (1707–1788), a forerunner of evolutionary theory, Diderot arrived at a conception of nature more dynamic than that of most of his fellow *philosophes*. Buffon had claimed that classifications are not realities of nature, but rather are constructs imposed on it by the mind. He objected to scientists, like Carl Linnaeus (1707–1779) and Charles Bonnet (1720–1793), who forced the realities of nature, its infinite variety and life process "which always proceeds by gradations," into a mechanistic system of abstract classification. Diderot espoused this view in his *On the Interpretation of Nature* (1754): "Everything changes and everything passes away; only the whole endures. The world is forever beginning and ending; each instant is its first and last; it never has had, never will have, any other beginning or end. In this vast ocean of matter, not one molecule is like another, no molecule is for one moment like itself. 'A new order of things is born': this is its eternal motto."

The world is in a constant state of flux; it is "a swift succession of things which follow each other, thrust forward and disappear; a transient symmetry; a momentary order." Heterogeneity, not uniformity, is the essential characteristic of nature. Nature is comprised of a mass of transient individualities; the basic category for understanding it, then, must be the whole, for "only the whole endures." Nothing in nature, including man, exists or can be understood apart from the whole. All things are conjoined in a hierarchy of being, and man, while he is at the top of the scale, stands in a relation of solidarity with this dynamic totality. "Every animal is more or less a man; every mineral is more or less a plant; every plant more or less an animal. . . . Since there is no quality of which no being has a share, it is the greater or less degree of this quality that makes us attribute it to one being to the exclusion of another." The parts of nature are mutable and can be understood only in relation to the ever-changing whole. "Change the world, and you will necessarily change me," Diderot writes in his *D'Alembert's Dream* (1769), "but the whole is constantly changing. . . . Man is merely a common product, the monster an uncommon product; both equally natural, equally necessary, equally part of the universal and general order of things."

Diderot's thinking had important new implications. His view of nature as a great creative process, of which man is an integral part, provided a middle term between the fact of necessity and the ideal of freedom. Man is embedded in nature, and nature determines all human behavior. But this determinism is progressive and creative in that it motivates man to realize his peculiarly human potentialities. This exalted conception, with its Aristotelian overtones, found its way into the thinking of Lessing and Goethe, both of whom were admirers of Diderot. His stress on the relativity of things meant that everything has some justification, while nothing has any absolute justification, except the whole. By stressing the interaction and interrelationship of the parts of nature with respect to the whole, Diderot broadened the scope of contemporary materialist philosophy and undermined its abstractness. Finally, nothing could do more to cast doubt on the existing order than the conclusion that the necessity of change is the eternal motto of nature: "A new world is born."

Diderot represented not only a new kind of thinking but also a new type of personality: the bohemian. In his early life at least, he preferred the cafes to the academies, the streets to the salons, leisure to a steady position—always the possible to the conventional. The tendency toward bohemianism, which culminated in Rousseau and his successors, was symptomatic of a new spirit in open protest against the bourgeoisie as well as against the aristocracy. It was Diderot alone who saw the *Encyclopedia* through to its completion, suffering imprisonment and countless setbacks in the process, but neither withdrawing his support out of fear or discouragement, as others did, nor heeding the advice of Voltaire, (who managed to make his peace with the system,) to emigrate and finish it abroad. In his clever, satirical novel, *Jacques the Fatalist*, the philosopher is not the dim-witted master, but rather the shrewd and easygoing valet. It is Jacques who observes: "The needy man doesn't walk like other people; he jumps, he crawls, he wriggles, he pulls himself along, he passes his life striking one pose after another. . . . In the entire kingdom, there is only one man who can walk upright; that is the sovereign. All the rest strike poses." But nowhere is the affinity of this new spirit and new type of personality more evident than in Diderot's novel of the sixties, *Rameau's Nephew*, in which the eccentric, nonconformist dilettante is set over against the professional bourgeois purveyor of the conventional wisdom.

This novel, like *D'Alembert's Dream* and *Jacques the Fatalist*, is written in the form of a witty dialogue. In all three writings, the center of interest is less the conclusions arrived at than the language; its tempo and humor, the dialectical manner of argumentation, and the tensions it produces. Hegel saw in the "universal talk and devastating judgment" of this novel a sign of "self-estrangement," the eighteenth-century philosophical mind struggling, by debunking everything, to gain mastery over and thus liberate itself from a crushing, contradictory reality. The sense of self-estrangement, "the inversion and perversion of all conceptions and realities," is indeed the keynote of the dialogue. Virtue, as represented by the respectable philosopher, reveals itself as vice, while vice, in the person of Rameau, reveals itself as virtue. The dialectic of this "game of dissolution that is played with itself" (Hegel) is grounded in Diderot's critique of contemporary society. The philosopher praises virtue but acquiesces in the evil practices of the world. The abject Rameau eulogizes vice, but in doing so, mercilessly unmasks the corruption of society. "And where does fulfilling one's duty lead to?" he asks. "To jealousy, trouble, persecution. Is that how one gets on in the world? No, good heavens, but by playing the courtier, frequenting great people, studying their tastes, humoring their whims, pandering to their vices, subscribing to their unjust actions —there's the secret." In spite of his egoism and immorality, however, Rameau finds himself lamenting "that torment of the conscience which springs from the uselessness of the gifts that Heaven has alloted to us, the most cruel of all torments. A man might almost as well not have been born." This sense of self-estrangement was the starting point of Rousseau.

Rousseau as the First "Modern" Man

If any single man is entitled to be called the first "modern" man, it is Jean-Jacques Rousseau (1712–1778). Not only was he a highly original thinker whose influence extended in every direction, but his formulation of the problem of civilization was so comprehensive and profound that it is relevant even today. Ever since the Renaissance, European culture had prided itself on its inherent worth; now a voice was heard to challenge this belief, proclaiming that there was something fundamentally false in the whole development. The betrayal of man by history and a plan for his resurrection through history was Rousseau's message. In his *Confessions* (1783), he portrays himself as a man of good instincts, good intentions, and friendly disposition driven to knavery, misanthropy, and eccentric behavior by the falsity and artificiality of society. He wrote the *Confessions* in fact believing that this portrayal was *typical* of most men ruined by an unjust and unequal society. He says in the introduction: "Let the numberless legion of my fellow men gather round me and hear my confessions. Let them groan at my depravities and bleed for my misdeeds. But let each of them reveal his heart at the foot of thy throne with equal sincerity, and may any man who dare, say 'I was a better man than he.'" Each of Rousseau's works sought to explain and remedy this general ruin and humiliation of mankind. Each of his attacks on society, each proposal he made for its transformation, sprang from his own conception of himself as typifying the human condition. In the course of his life, as he increasingly withdrew into himself and became a friendless wanderer, he felt that he alone was just,

authentic, truly alive; that history and society, the per-
verters of the rest of mankind, would betray him also if he
abandoned his solitude. In turning away from the world,
however, he hoped to preserve in his own being what was
best in humanity at large.

Rousseau and the Problem of Culture

Rousseau's first work of importance, *Discourse on the
Arts and Sciences* (1750), was written for an essay contest
held by the Academy of Dijon in answer to the question
concerning the moral effects of culture on human character.
Whether it was Rousseau's own idea to take the negative
side of the question, or whether he did so at Diderot's sug-
gestion, as has been claimed, there is no doubt that he was
perplexed at this time by what he considered to be a glaring
contradiction between the inner world of feeling and the
whole of contemporary culture. "What happiness would it
be for those who live among us, if our external appearance
were always a mirror of our hearts; if decorum were but
virtue; if the maxims we professed were the rules of our
conduct; and if real philosophy were inseparable from the
title of a philosopher!" Rousseau attributed this contradiction
to culture itself which degraded men by estranging them
from themselves and from one another. Before the appearances of the arts and sciences, man's morals were "rude but
natural. . . . Human nature was not at bottom better then
than now; but men found their security in the ease with
which they could see through one another, and this advantage, of which we no longer feel the value, prevented their
having many vices." The depravity came with culture.
"Where there is no effect, it is idle to look for a cause: but

here the effect is certain and the depravity actual; our minds have been corrupted in proportion as the arts and sciences have been improved."

Rousseau was mistaken in regarding culture as the cause of moral depravity, when both are actually the effects of more basic social and political forces. This error he corrected in his later writings. But he was the first to see at work in culture the same forces at work in society at large; the first to see that the problem of culture is the problem of society itself. The very fact that he mistakenly considered culture in this discourse to be the *cause* of moral corruption indicates how forcefully he was impressed by its power to corrupt. The arts, literature, and the sciences, he recognized, can sanction social and political despotism if they "stifle in men's breasts that sense of original liberty, for which they seem to have been born; cause them to love their own slavery, and so make of them what is called a civilized people." This novel view, which was more justified than anyone was willing to admit (supporters of the Old Regime and critics alike), obviously flew in the face of the intellectualistic trend of the Enlightenment and earned Rousseau the hostility of his fellow *philosophes*, particularly that of Voltaire. In fact, he was simply applying the critical ideals of the Enlightenment to itself.

Rousseau and the Problem of Society

What Rousseau meant by moral corruption was precisely the self-estrangement of modern man, an evil consisting in the aforementioned discrepancy between the inner and outer man. He contrasted this discrepancy, which he thought to be the essential characteristic of civilized man, to the consistency and organic unity of primitive man. This contrast is fundamental to Rousseau's social philosophy. But it is important to note that he did not praise primitive man as such. On the contrary, he explicity denied that human nature was better then than now. What he praised in primitive man was solely the transparency of his nature which acts as a curb to vice. Where men "can see through one another," look into each other's hearts, deception is difficult and also unnecessary. Conversely, where men seem opaque to one another, where the inner self manifests itself only obliquely, if at all, deception and vice are easy, irresistible, and also indispensable to survival. Rousseau thus anticipated Freud in characterizing modern man as being basically at odds with himself, although Rousseau took into account that human psychology changes in and through history, and therefore limited himself to characterizing *only* modern European man in this way. He feared that where external appearance is not "a true mirror of our hearts," it tends to suppress or swallow up the inner self. The result is a unidimensional being who is no longer capable of self-determination but who is necessarily subject to control from without. Rousseau was not a primitivist, but rather a humanist eager to define the conditions essential to freedom. He praised the transparency of primitive man not because it was primitive (although he did suppose that it once existed), but because it signalized to him a human wholeness in contrast to the character of modern man whose appearance, however consistent in itself, seemed so divested of inner motivation that it threatened to consume his entire being.

> In our day, now that more subtle study, and a more refined taste have reduced the art of pleasing to a system, there prevails in modern manners a servile and deceptive conformity; so that one would think every mind had been

cast in the same mould. Politeness requires this thing; decorum that; ceremony has its forms, and fashion its laws, and these we must always follow, never the promptings of our own nature.

We no longer dare seem what we really are, but lie under a perpetual constraint; in the meantime the herd of men, which we call society, all act under the same circumstances exactly alike, unless very particular and powerful motives prevent them. Thus we never know with whom we have to deal; and even to know our friends we must wait for some critical and pressing occasion; that is, till it is too late; for it is on those very occasions that such knowledge is of use to us. (*Discourse on the Arts and Sciences.*)

In conjunction with his critique of culture, Rousseau began to place a new emphasis on the value of the emotions, an emphasis for which Hume's negative limitation of reason prepared the way. His own ideas, he reveals in the *Confessions*, were usually born of his emotions. In moments of solitude, his heart sometimes swelled to such fulness that he could scarcely express himself. Then he had difficulty finding concepts adequate to his feelings. Such personal experiences taught him that feeling is just as original and significant a side of inner life as the intellect, that feeling is not merely passive and receptive in relation to reason, and that the two, in contrast to Prévost's view, need not be mutually antagonistic. Feeling was important because it exercised a formative influence on reason itself. But Rousseau did not defend feeling *against* reason, any more than he asserted the superiority of primitive man as such over civilized man. What he sought to express was a conception of harmony and human wholeness based on the spontaneity of the emotions. His position on the function of feeling within the totality of spiritual life is stated very clearly in his second writing of importance, the *Discourse on the Origin of Inequality* (1755):

> Whatever moralists may hold, the human understanding is greatly indebted to the passions, which, it is universally allowed, are also much indebted to the understanding. It is by the activity of the passions that our reason is improved; for we desire knowledge only because we wish to enjoy; and it is impossible to conceive any reason why a person who has neither fears nor desires should give himself the trouble of reasoning. The passions, again, originate in our wants, and their progress depends on that of our knowledge; for we cannot desire or fear anything, except from the idea we have of it, or from the simple impulse of nature.

This view was not new to the Enlightenment; Voltaire, Diderot, and Hume all fully believed that the passions are basic to the functioning of reason. But Rousseau's emphasis on them had a new and socially radical implication. In his reaction to contemporary culture, he turned to the basic and primary relations of life: love, friendship, and the solace of an uncorrupted nature. These commanded his respect and brought him what irregular joy he ever knew. He found something in these relations common to all men, regardless of the differences in their intellectual competence. In according primacy to them, he found himself speaking on behalf of those whom the encyclopedists regarded as stragglers in the march of civilization and whom Voltaire referred to as *canaille*. Rousseau differed from these other *philosophes* in that he looked to the cultivation of a relationship which would embrace all men as the only way to heal the discord between the inner and outer self. This he found in the love of virtue, the principles of which are "graven on every heart." For him, as for Montesquieu, love of virtue, by restoring the unity of man, could serve as the basis for what they both considered to be the only true culture—a culture of citizenship. However, Rousseau's radically democratic formulation of this view was bound to come into conflict with the realities of bourgeois utilitarianism as well as with those of aristocratic exclusionism. For, according to him, man was corrupted in the first place precisely because private privilege and unrestrained self-seeking since antiquity had been allowed to stifle and supplant the public realm of life. "The politicians of the ancient world were always talking of morals and virtue; ours speak of nothing but commerce and money. . . . let them [our politicians] learn for once that money, though it buys everything else, cannot buy morals and citizens." He recognized, even in the first discourse, that the culture and politics of his day stood in diametrical opposition to each other to the detriment of each. "So long as power alone is on one side, and knowledge and understanding alone on the other, the learned will seldom make great objects their study, princes will still more rarely perform great actions, and the peoples will continue to be, as they are, mean, corrupt, and miserable." The second discourse is devoted to an historical analysis of this situation.

Here Rousseau attributes the moral corruption of man by culture to the substitution of social and civilized life for the state of nature. His use of the term "state of nature," however, is mainly hypothetical. It is a concept with which he sought to distinguish between "what is original and what is artificial in the actual nature of man." He defines it as "a state which no longer exists, perhaps never did exist, and probably never will exist; and of which it is nevertheless necessary to have true ideas in order to form a proper judgment of our present state." Rousseau was still very much within the tradition of natural law, but his idea of the state of nature differed substantially from that of his predecessors, Grotius, Hobbes, and Locke. He criticizes them for having erroneously attributed virtues and vices to mankind even before the existence of organized society, and for having called "natural," therefore, what was really a set of characteristics man acquired in a civil state. Thus he believed that they took to be original what was actually artificial in the nature of man. The result was that natural law, and the rights commonly derived from it, turned out to be not a true explanation of "the nature of things," but rather an arbitrary justification for this or that set of particular interests. "Modern writers begin by inquiring what rules it would be expedient for men to agree on for their common interest, and then give the name of natural law to a collection of these rules without any other proof than the good that would result from their being universally followed." Not wishing to fall into the error of making "man a philosopher before he is a man," Rousseau denied that man in the state of nature was either moral or immoral, terms which could have no meaning with respect to a condition in which men were isolated and indifferent to one another. Likewise, there was no harmony, and no need of harmony, between self-interest and the general good in the state of nature. By eliminating all those characteristics which he believed man acquired in and through society (and this included almost everything), Rousseau discovered only two principles of the human soul "prior to reason": the instinct of self-preservation, and a certain capacity to sympathize with suffering. Working initially within the tradition of natural law, he thus succeeded in exposing its abstract and ideological character, and in breaking through to a critical-historical approach to the study of man.

Rousseau calls the state of nature the period of human evolution from primitive isolation to the agricultural phase. During this time, under the pressure of a growing population, and by their ability to learn from experience, men began to cooperate in satisfying their needs, and in doing so, learned the rudiments of morality. So long as there was plenty for all, there was no need of private property and no social conflict. So long as men were independent of each other, slavery was impossible and freedom natural. Everyone was his own master and no one could impose on others the law of the strongest. The last stage in this development was the happiest and most stable, "a period of expansion of the human faculties, keeping a just mean between the indolence of the primitive state and the petulant activity of our egoism. . . ."

But this final phase, in allowing man leisure to invent "conveniences unknown to his fathers," enabled him inadvertently to impose on himself his first yoke. For these conveniences soon degenerated into indispensable needs. The occasion soon came when, for the first time, someone enclosed a piece of ground and "bethought himself of saying, 'This is mine,' and found people simple enough to believe him." He was the true founder of civil society. The act by which it was founded was not, therefore, a considered political contract, as Rousseau's predecessors believed, but rather an unexpected social act which led to the corruption of mankind. For men could have spared themselves untold misery if someone had cried: "Beware of listening to this imposter; you are undone if you once forget that the fruits of the earth belong to us all, and the earth itself to nobody." By this time, however, the equilibrium between human wants and the capacity to satisfy them was disrupted anyway. From this original evil followed all other evils. The establishment of private property simply delivered the final blow to the relative equality of the state of nature. Those inequalities which did exist, due to natural differences and harmless in the state of nature, evolved into serious social inequalities. As wealth was now inheritable, social classes developed, with the richest tyrannizing over the rest. Thus freedom disappeared along with equality.

The introduction of private property also gave rise to the moral evils characteristic of civilized man. The instinct of self-preservation (*amour de soi*) evolved into egoism (*amour propre*) which finds satisfaction at the expense of others. This is how self-estrangement came about. "It now became the interest of men to appear what they really were not. To be and to seem became two totally different things; and from this distinction sprang insolent pomp and cheating trickery, with all the numerous vices that go in their train. . . . In a word, there arose rivalry and competition on the one hand, and conflicting interests on the other, together with a secret desire on both of profiting at the expense of others. All these evils were the first effects of property, and the inseparable attendants of growing inequality." Men no longer worked to satisfy their real wants, but rather to get more than others. Permanent war developed between rich and poor. But since this war was not in the interest of the wealthy, the rich man "conceived at length the profoundest plan that ever entered the mind of man: this was to employ in his favor the forces of those who attacked him, to make allies of his adversaries, to inspire them with different maxims, and to give them other institutions as favorable to himself as the law of nature was unfavorable." In such a society, it was nonsense to speak of a natural harmony of interests. The poor lost their freedom and gained nothing;

the rich, "having feelings . . . in every part of their pos-
sessions," invented civil society to sanction and protect their
property.

It is clear from all this why Rousseau thought that
culture corrupted mankind. In a civilization which stood in
need not merely of reform, but rather was rotten to the core,
rotten in its very inception, culture, as the expression of its
values, could only serve to sustain what needed to be overthrown. Society, in his view, far from being a continuation
and refinement of the state of nature, as Locke had maintained, offered only the spectacle of "an assembly of artificial men and factitious passions, which are the work of all
these new relations, and without any real foundation in
nature. . . . We have nothing to show for ourselves but a
frivolous and deceitful appearance, honor without virtue,
reason without wisdom, and pleasure without happiness."
Whereas the savage "breathes only peace and liberty," civilized man is always "moving, sweating, toiling. . . . The
savage lives within himself, while social man lives constantly
outside himself, and knows only how to live in the opinion
of others, so that he seems to receive the consciousness of
his own existence merely from the judgments of others
concerning him . . ."

Yet Rousseau did not believe that a return to nature
was either possible or desirable. For one thing, moral corruption had gone too far for that. For another, he never lost
sight of the mainly hypothetical character of the state of
nature he purported to describe. Finally, he must have had
his doubts about a lost paradise which, if it ever did exist,
proved unable to withstand the forces working for its destruction. Rousseau was not a revolutionary, preferring to
believe that the hand that wounds is the hand that heals. If
history was responsible for man's self-estrangement, and if

humanity could not revert to its former ideal state, then history had to have a new beginning, which would enable man to return to himself by recovering his lost unity at a higher level of existence. To this end, Rousseau claimed that the individual needed a new sort of education, and humanity as a whole a new political constitution. *Emile* (1762) was his proposal for an education which would encourage the individual to develop "naturally." His *Discourse on Political Economy* (1755) and *The Social Contract* (1762) were proposals for a political constitution which would enable the individual to develop his personality in accordance with the principle of social equality. Far from being a pessimist with regard to the future, he believed that men, without having recourse to revolution, could realize their potentiality for self-perfection. And because this potentiality came from nature and constituted what was original in human nature, it was bound to triumph ultimately over intellectual pride and the falsity of existing social relations which formed the artificial side of his nature.

Rousseau and the Problem of Politics

Rousseau no longer concerned himself in *The Social Contract* with how the transition from the state of nature to civil society came about. He notes only that it produced "a very remarkable change in man, by substituting justice for instinct in his conduct, and giving his actions the morality they had formerly lacked." Here he was concerned, like Montesquieu, with what could make this transition legitimate, "men being taken as they are and laws as they might be." Both natural law and force are rejected as the basis of legitimate authority. The first mistakenly seeks to justify authority in terms of an actual state of nature which no longer exists. The second is no justification at all, since by subordinating right to force it destroys the very foundation of legitimacy. "The problem is to find a form of association which will defend and protect with the whole common force the person and goods of each associate, and in which each, while uniting himself with all, may still obey himself alone, and remain as free as before." The advantage of this sort of association is that "each man, in giving himself to all, gives himself to nobody; and as there is no associate over which he does not acquire the same rights as he yields others over himself, he gains an equivalent for everything he loses, and an increase of force for the preservation of what he has."

This association is the only one which would justify, and more than justify, the transition from nature to society; all would gain and no one would lose. The only valid authority for such an association would be that to which each and every individual voluntarily submits—authority founded on freedom. The renunciation of freedom, Rousseau says, "is incompatible with man's nature; to remove all liberty from his will is to remove all morality from his acts." Freedom, then, is *natural* to man, and in order for him to retain it in the civil state, he must have recourse to justice rather than to instinct. The paradox here is that in order to retain what is natural to him, man must avail himself of *un*natural or *post*natural means. Justice is not natural, but it enables man to preserve what is and to live in accordance with nature. Freedom and law, therefore, are indissolubly linked. The preservation of freedom requires the creation of an inviolable law; but it is a law which every person, acting in concert with all, enacts for himself. This strict correlation of freedom and law, by which natural man becomes truly social, became the basis of Rousseau's conception of the general will.

The general will only finds expression in a system of laws to which all men freely submit. Since law is universal by definition, the general will cannot simply represent the will of the majority, nor even the sum of all individual wills. To identify the general will with the sum of private wills would be tantamount, in Rousseau's view, to accepting Bernard Mandeville's thesis, as put forth in the *Fable of the Bees* (1714), that the pursuit of private interests makes for the public good. But since Mandeville himself recognized that self-seeking only refines its motive force, egoism, the ideal form of assocation envisaged by Rousseau could not possibly result from it. What Rousseau meant by the general will was something qualitatively different from the private will. The one differs from the other as justice differs from instinct. The private will is simply the manifestation of instinct in the civil state and can have no other result than the "public good" in the cynical sense of Mandeville.

Thus, Rousseau took care to distinguish between the "will of all," which "takes private interest into account," and the general will which "considers only the common interest." The first is merely public opinion, the latter public spirit—what Montesquieu meant by virtue. The general will is general not because it represents the will of the many, but rather because its object is general: the general good. In the good society, of course, it would represent the will of the many also. The point is, however, that the general will does not completely cease to be, even if nobody expresses it. On the other hand, it is only fully operative when it is actually held in common. The general will requires both good government and self-government; neither is really possible without the other.

Rousseau defined the common good as "liberty and equality—liberty, because all particular dependence means so much force taken from the body of the State, and equality, because liberty cannot exist without it." In order that the common good might be realized, Rousseau insisted on "the total alienation of each associate, together with all his rights, to the whole community; for, in the first place, as each man gives himself absolutely, the conditions are the same for all; and, this being so, no one has any interest in making them burdensome to others." The reason for this total alienation was that, if individuals retained certain rights, "each, being on one point his own judge, would ask to be so on all; the state of nature would thus continue, and the association would necessarily become inoperative and tyrannical." Rousseau advocated the total sovereignty of the state, but this sovereignty presupposed that the state would be guided solely by the general will. If the state exercised total sovereignty without being so guided, it would forfeit its legitimacy. The good society, for Rousseau, was a democratic egalitarian republic.

As this form of association comes into being, it becomes natural to man, replacing the state of nature. Freedom is no longer merely the absence of restraint, as those believed, like Locke, who regarded civil society as the perpetuation and guarantee of the state of nature under the protection of government. For Rousseau, freedom in society meant interaction and active fellowship among men; a positive sociablenesss which was absent in the state of nature. This freedom would be possible only on condition of relative economic equality. For no rights, including property rights, are prior to the community; and since the individual finds fulfillment only in the community, inequality is fatal to both. Just as Rousseau recognized that a people becomes a people before it gives itself a government, that government is the creation of society and has no independent existence or vested rights whatever, except where it usurps them, so too he recognized that liberty, the prime political right, depends on equality, the prime social right. In this respect, as in his democratic leanings generally, Rousseau did not so much differ from the other enlighteners as carry their thinking to its logical conclusion. He insisted that the liberation of the bourgeoisie is not equivalent to the liberation of all mankind, that no man can be free until all men are, and that the good society cannot be good just for some but must be good for all.

The sovereignty of the people, inalienable individual rights, and legal equality were all written into the *Declaration of the Rights of Man and of the Citizen* (1789). In respect to property, however, the moderate formulators of the *Declaration,* fearful of the egalitarian demands of the more democratic radicals, frightened by the prospect of a mass uprising, and anxious to appease the property owning class to which they belonged, followed Locke rather than Rousseau, declaring property a sacred and inalienable "natural" right. This document, which went so far as to repudiate the existing feudal hierarchy, but not so far as to defend social democracy, favored instead a constitutional monarchy based on a propertied elite expressing itself through a representative assembly.

Rousseau's social theory marked a shift in the center of gravity of the Enlightenment. It gave expression to an all-pervasive sense of disillusionment which developed rapidly after mid-century, the disillusionment felt by a jaded aristocracy, an irritated and bewildered bourgeoisie, an oppressed peasantry and an urban lower class, and by an emerging German intellectual proletariat. The upper-class

cult of primitivism and lower-class utopian socialism, theories of extreme individualism and extreme collectivism, the
rigorously rational idealism of Kant and the equally rigorous
emotional idealism of the "Storm and Stress" movement—
all found inspiration in Rousseau. His thinking, sometimes
melancholy and sometimes apocalyptic, inspired the idea of
nature as innocence lost. Just as Pascal, a century earlier,
had sounded the loss of God, Rousseau now pronounced the
loss of nature. Self-estranged man, for him, was the "de-
natured" social man of his time, the man who never follows
the promptings of his own nature, but rather "lives constantly outside himself, and knows only how to live in the
opinion of others." The general will was intended to *substitute* for the state of nature, to provide a standard of justice
and a norm for political action, and thus eventually lead to
the recovery of nature. But, in fact, the idea of nature as
lost innocence aroused in the aristocrats, living out their
overrefined and formal lives at court, and in the city-dwelling
bourgeois, who still lived to such a great extent in the image
of the aristocracy, the memory of a mythical Eden. Nature
became for them a symbol of Paradise Lost, and they imag-
ined they could reawaken the memory of it by a "return
to nature," by idealizing the peasant and adoring the coun-
tryside. However, by surrounding the rustic life in a halo of
pristine happiness and idyllic simplicity, this primitivism
had the dual effect of undermining the self-confidence of the
upper classes, and of giving support to the social hierarchy.
Not only primitivism, however, but all the movements which
found inspiration in Rousseau were just so many attempts,
whether sterile or fruitful, whether reactionary or progressive, to cope with the sense of the loss of nature. At one
extreme we find an outright revolt against nature; at the
other a new humanistic rehabilitation of it.

THE LIMITS OF ENLIGHTENMENT: DECLINE AND TRANSITION

The Revolt Against Nature: Sade as Nihilist

Immanuel Kant (1724–1804) and the Marquis de Sade (1740–1814) form the positive and negative poles respectively of the revolt against nature. Sade is significant in the history of the Enlightenment for having shown that the philosophy of nature on which deism was founded, and from which the amiable La Mettrie and the well-meaning Holbach had derived a utilitarian ethics and social theory, leads just as consistently to nihilism. His writings and twisted life (twenty-seven years of which were spent in prisons and asylums) were devoted to proving, quite consciously *en philosophe,* that in the realm of ethics if nature sanctions everything, it sanctions nothing. Nature, in its very omnipotence, is amoral, meaningless, totally indifferent to man. In his notorious novel, *Juliette* (1796), he writes: "The relations of man to nature, or of nature to man, are . . . nil; nature cannot chain man by any law; man does not depend on nature in any way, they owe nothing to each

101

other, and can neither offend each other nor serve each other. Once he is launched, man is free from nature. . . ."

This view obviously undercut the characteristic Enlightenment sanction for morality, although it did not in itself necessarily imply that man should be immoral or unjust. But Sade went farther. Nature is not merely amoral; in its very indifference it is positively immoral, a great metaphysical joke perpetrated against mankind. That nature did *not* provide any moral norm is what enraged Sade. His grotesque obsession with the fact that the cosmos is altogether silent with regard to human conduct echoed the profound disorientation of many during the French Revolution, when he began to be read. Utilitarianism had proclaimed that if man lived according to nature he would be both virtuous and happy. Nature, for Sade, might sanction happiness, but virtue never. "Nothing is more immoral than nature; it never imposed any limits on us, never dictated any laws. . . ." If nature prescribes anything, it is extreme egoism and nihilism. Contrary to utilitarian theory, the instinctual urge to happiness and the ideal of social harmony are not merely disunited but sharply antithetical.

Sade concluded that both the acceptance and the denial of nature leads to crime. Since nothing in nature is moral, it is meaningless even to distinguish between vice and virtue or between crime and justice. The condemnation of crime is itself a crime committed by the strong against the weak in defense of an arbitrary social system; a conspiracy designed to keep the strong strong, the weak weak. Even the virtuous Rousseau had regarded what passed for justice as a part of that "profoundest plan that ever entered the mind of man," a plan whereby the rich man persuaded the poor to accept maxims and institutions "as favorable to himself as the law of nature was unfavorable." In the eyes of both Rousseau and Sade, it was society that made men subservient to forces for which there was no moral justification whatever. Rousseau himself might almost have written the following passage which actually appears in Sade's *Justine* (1791):

> What is virtue if it cannot prevent the tyranny of the strong over the weak, or the rich over the poor, or those who are in power over those who are not in power! Filled with the will for power, the voices of virtue forge irons with which to chain men. And men, stupified by their misery, willingly believe everything told them. Can virtue, sprung from such motives, win our respect? Is there a single truth which does not bear the mark of falsehood and lies? What do we find in them: mysteries that cause reason to shudder; dogmas that outrage nature; and ceremonies that inspire only disgust and derision!

Sade's revolt was directed in the first place against society in the name of the injustice of both God and nature. The only meaningful course of action he could conceive was to turn the very forces by which the strong became strong —those "mysteries that cause reason to shudder; dogmas that outrage nature; and ceremonies that inspire only disgust and derision"—against the strong themselves. Since virtue is simply the ideology of the strong, freedom requires that it be subverted. "Don't you see that the cruelty of the rich forces the poor to rebel! Why don't they open their purses to our needs? Let humanity rule their hearts, then virtue will rule ours! . . . We are all created free and equal by nature; but if chance puts out of order this first law of nature, is it not up to us to correct its caprices by our strength and numbers? . . . Would you have us abstain from crime and murder, which alone can open the gates of life to us? As long as this class domineers over us we'll remain degraded, in want and tears!" In an unjust universe, in which happiness and virtue are antithetical, Sade's revolt took the form of crime, the only sort of revolt, he believed, which is consistent with nature and which also brings with it happiness. His was an intellectual joy in moral regression, an *amor intellectualis diaboli,* arising out of a lust to smash a hypocritical society with its own weapons. "Nature wills it thus. When her secret workings make us do evil it is because evil is necessary to her scheme. Let no one be frightened or hindered if his soul forces him to do evil. Let him commit crimes without regrets as soon as he feels the necessity! It is only by resisting such an urge that men act against nature."

But Sade finally extended his revolt to nature itself as the ultimate source of all evil. Since the one and only rule of nature is "that of attaining happiness, no matter at whose expense," the act which gives the greatest pleasure is also the most worthwhile. This was the thinking behind Sade's obsession with sex, although he was obsessed even more with sexual perversity. Sex, for him, not only yielded the greatest pleasure, but as the realm in which nature most closely touches man in his relations with others, it was here that he could hope to violate nature itself, insult it for its immoral indifference to man. Exercising absolute power over another human being in the sex act, affirming his own existence in it by denying that of another gave him the satisfaction of outraging nature. In the last analysis, crime seemed to him always "sublime and triumphant" less because it was consistent with nature than because it was a gesture in defiance of nature. As such, it seemed to him to be a supremely free and godlike act comparable to creation itself. "It is nature I long to be able to outrage. I want to throw its plans into disorder and block its ordained movements, to arrest the stars in their course and shake the globes which float in cosmic space, to destroy what serves nature and give protection to what irritates it—in a word, to insult nature and suspend its great effects."

This supreme crime, the violation of nature, was to Sade the epitome of human freedom. But, for all of his satanism, even he recognized the hopelessness of committing it: "The impossibility of outraging nature is, in my opinion, the greatest anguish man can know." So Sade contented himself with committing the lesser crimes of which he was capable. Once it is admitted that man cannot destroy nature, however, it follows that the only other way to take vengeance on it—and this is the *reductio ad absurdum* of sadism —is precisely to practice virtue, as this would satisfy the sadistic requirement of transgression. But in a world in which all agreed that no justice existed, virtue was bound to appear to most men, in Sade's words, as "always sad and sulking, pedantic and unfortunate," a sentiment re-echoed by his contemporary, Choderlos de Laclos, in his *Les Liaisons Dangereuses*. Despite the obvious illogic of his position, Sade did succeed in exposing the ideological implications of utilitarianism. By showing that nature no more forbids crime than sanctions virtue, he blasted the utilitarian reconciliation of natural necessity and human freedom, of happiness and virtue. Sade's importance lies less in his grotesque thinking, however, than in the grim, caricatural image he held up to a society which had lost nature as a moral norm, and with it, confidence in morality itself.

The Revolt Against "Nature": Kant as Moralist

Kant represents the positive pole of the revolt against nature. For him, as for Sade, nature and virtue are antithetical, and this anthesis is responsible for the "conflict between the natural and the moral species" within man. Both considered this conflict as basic and inevitable. But, whereas Sade accorded primacy to nature, even when he diabolically longed to destroy it, Kant drew the conclusion that Sade logically should have drawn; namely, that the practice of virtue alone enables man to defy nature. Rather than lashing out at nature in blind rage, Kant followed Rousseau in maintaining that it is in fact natural for social man to reject nature. "Nature has willed that man should, by himself, produce everything that goes beyond the mechanical ordering of his animal existence. . . ." Virtue, for Kant, is not prescribed by nature; it supplants nature. So rigorous was his conception of virtue that he suspected any allegedly moral act which simultaneously would satisfy a natural urge. In his treatise entitled *The Metaphysics of Morals* (1797), he writes:

> Virtue is the strength of a man's maxims in following his duty. All strength is known by the obstacles which it can overcome; with virtue, these are the natural inclinations, which can come into conflict with the moral prescription; and since it is man himself who puts these obstacles in the way of his maxims, virtue is not only compulsion of oneself . . . but a compulsion according to a principle of inner freedom.

Kant's Critique of Pure Reason

Kant's point of departure was the philosophy of Hume who, as we have seen, claimed that our concepts are not given in experience and have no necessary relation to reality; rather they are the product of the psychological process of association. Kant, in his first great philosophical work, *Critique of Pure Reason* (1781), undertook to reexamine the relationship of knowledge to reality. If our concepts are not given in experience but are formed by the mind, can they, he asked, still be valid for things which are entirely independent of us? On the other hand, if experience is our only source of knowledge, as Locke and the French materialists had maintained, how was the mind able to form concepts, like causality, which seemed to transcend experience? According to Kant, knowledge must be valid of things, yet by either theory it seems that it cannot be. For while the objects of knowledge to which these concepts apply are only objects given in sense experience, sense experience does not provide the concepts with which the mind does in fact transform experience into knowledge. Knowledge, for Kant, is a unified process involving the cooperation of perception (intuition), imagination, and understanding: ". . . neither concepts without an intuition corresponding to them, nor intuitions without concepts can yield any real knowledge."

Kant did not mean that the mind imposes arbitrary ideas or moods on nature. He did mean that all experience presupposes a general and necessary capacity of the mind to unite, combine, and relate (synthesize) sense impressions. Kant postulated this view on the grounds that there is a constant and universal element in knowledge which does not derive from sense impressions, since these vary and are always in flux. Space and time, for example, are not properties of things but rather necessary and invariant modes of perception. They are not received from sensations but are contributed to sensations by the perceiving mind. Space and time, therefore, are logically independent of and prior to sense impressions. What appears in space and time Kant calls phenomena; nature is "phenomena under law," and knowledge is possible because the mind prescribes the laws (of space, time, causality, etc.) under which the phenomena are experienced. For these laws are the laws of the mind's own working in "deciphering appearances in order to read them as [objects of] experience." This process of "deciphering appearances" (or synthesis) occurs in three stages: sensations are transformed into perceptions within the forms of space and time (which are not given in sensation); perceptions are transformed into experience by means of concepts of the understanding (e.g., cause, substance, reality, possibility, and necessity, which are not given in perception); experience, which is not just a collection of isolated bits of information, is raised to systematic knowledge by means of general principles which Kant calls Ideas (e.g., the soul, the world, and God, which are not given in experience). We can know nature, which is the appearance of reality as structured by these operations of mind. But we cannot know metaphysical reality, since its laws may not be the same as those of mind. Metaphysical reality eludes us in our very effort to grasp it; but what we ordinarily, and in science, call reality (everything from sticks and stones to atoms and stars) we can know.

Thus Kant distinguished between appearance (the phenomenal world) and reality (the thing-in-itself or the noumenal world). The object of knowledge is nature as a phenomenon; as a thing-in-itself it is unknowable, only a hypothesis. The purpose of this distinction was to avoid the conclusion that nothing is real except what appears to man. If everything were resolved into phenomena, true knowledge, knowledge valid of experience but unconditioned by it (synthetic a priori knowledge), would be impossible. This was Hume's view. But, according to Kant, we do in fact

possess synthetic a priori knowledge, of which mathematics
is the best example; hence we are forced to distinguish between what we call nature and metaphysical reality, even
though we cannot know this reality in itself. Hume, in as-
serting the sovereignty of the empirical world, had reduced
knowledge to a strictly subjective status. Kant denied the
sovereignty of the empircal world in order to save the possibility of objective knowledge of it.

Superficially, it would seem that, by limiting reason,
by denying that it can know reality, Kant represents a departure from the Enlightenment tradition. Actually, his assertion of this limitation bolstered his faith in reason, because he believed that it stemmed from reason itself and is
known by reason's own laws. Philosophy, for him, was always
a question of defining the relationship between reason and
nature. By distinguishing between appearance and reality,
Kant tried to steer between the Scylla of materialism, which
explained life exclusively in terms of external influences,
and the Charybdis of metaphysics, which, whether in the
form of revealed religion, deism, mysticism, or pantheism,
sought to extend knowledge beyond its proper sphere, that
of experience. Like most of the enlighteners, he conceived
nature as a mechanistic system, governed strictly by the law
of cause and effect. But, since the empirical world could
not claim to be identical with reality (else *it* could not be
known), he believed that, in addition to knowledge of nature, freedom and morality also were still possible. The exploration of this possibility was the subject of his writings
on ethics, the *Foundations of the Metaphysics of Morals*
(1785) and the *Critique of Practical Reason* (1788).

Kant on Reason and Morality

Here Kant maintains that man is subject to the law of causality in so far as he belongs to the phenomenal world, but is free in that he also belongs to the noumenal world. In the *Foundations of the Metaphysics of Morals,* he writes: "Nothing can possibly be conceived in the world, or even out of it, which can be called good without qualification, except a good will." The good will cannot be conditioned by the law of nature; it must be free and self-determining. The will becomes good only when reason prescribes to it a universal and necessary moral law, a law which Kant calls a categorical imperative. One of the most important of these is: "Act as if the maxim from which you act were to become through your will a universal law of nature." If the moral law conflicts with the law of nature, the former takes precedence because the empirical world is not reality. Since the law of nature is only a construction we put on appearances, it is still possible that the moral law is realizable in the realm of reality. In any case, there is no contradiction in postulating the eventual attainment of the goals prescribed to us by the moral law. If man does not obey this law of his own making, Kant claims, it is not because the law of nature holds sway, but because man's will is weak and his disposition evil. If he is to obey the moral law, however, man must set himself in opposition to the deterministic world of nature. Struggling thus, moral man finds himself in revolt against nature. Whereas the misanthropic Sade despaired of the capacity of human malice to outrage nature, Kant considered the rejection of nature as the highest moral demand, one which is both possible and necessary to the moral progress of mankind.

Kant carried over this conception to his theory of history and society. History, for him, was the recounting of man's progress from the state of nature, in which he was a mere mechanism, to the state of culture, through which he liberates himself by becoming free and rational. But it was also a field of struggle between nature and morality, because "nature has given us two different dispositions for two different purposes, the one for man as an animal, the other for man as a moral species." The existence of this conflict, which was the source of what Kant called man's "unsocial sociality," caused him to renounce the possibility of human happiness in history. For he analyzed the problem of civilization thus:

> The real trouble is that, on the one hand, culture progressively interferes with its natural function, by altering the conditions to which it was suited, while on the other hand, natural impulse interferes with culture until such time as finally art will be strong enough to become second nature. This indeed is the ultimate moral end of the human species. (*Conjectural Beginning of Human History.*)

Although nature denies man the prospect of happiness, she does enable him to become "worthy of happiness" by endowing him with the ability to achieve "a universal civic society which administers law among men." The progress of reason will bring an increase in self-government. Kant's advocacy of republican government followed from his ethical theory. In society, as with the individual, morality is the rational expression of an autonomous, self-determining will. Through the struggle brought on by man's "unsocial sociability," humanity will move toward the realization of a world republic and eventually "perpetual peace." Nature, by disowning man, so to speak, forces him to become moral and to extend morality to politics and society in order to survive. We do not learn morality from history, but history does enable us to see how "the destiny of the race can be fulfilled here on earth."

This "destiny," however, is only an Idea, similar to an Idea in Plato's sense. Like Kant's other Ideas, the Idea of a genuine moral republic is an archetype, something which never existed, but which is created by the human mind to guide and regulate it toward this goal. The fulfillment of the Idea of history does not depend on history, but rather on freedom. The historical order, like the natural order, is only a construction we put on appearances—in this case, on the appearances of the past (e.g. documents, artifacts, etc.). And just as the moral law takes precedence over the law of nature, so too it must prevail over history, which Kant thought of as no more than "this idiotic course of things human." Some scattered indications in history suggest that mankind can progress; whether it will or not depends on men's free acts, not on any inference of the future from the past. At any given moment, man has a moral responsibility to act "as if" the Idea of history will be realized. Its realization depends exclusively on this moral stance, not on conclusions about the past drawn by historians. Like the blind necessity governing nature, the "idiotic" momentum of history can prevail only when morality breaks down. Conversely, every moral act represents a new beginning which is determined neither by nature nor by history. If history teaches us anything, it is only that the future does not depend on the past, but rather on the free actions of individuals in the present.

Ethics and Aesthetics in Kant's Thought

In his last great philosophical writing, the *Critique of Judgment* (1790), which combines the results of the first two *Critiques,* Kant sought to unite the originality and autonomy of the will with the empirical world as determined by the law of nature. Man lives and acts in nature but man can and should follow the law of freedom. The moral law, then, can only find expression in the world of experience. And Kant asks here if there is not after all something common to both nature and morality. To resolve the antithesis between natural determinism and freedom, without abandoning either, he shows that it is necessary to make use of the Idea of purpose. Even though nature does not in fact work according to purpose, we must regard it "as if" it did, so as to understand the purposeless mechanical relations according to which it actually does operate. It is especially in the realm of aesthetics that nature can be reconciled with freedom. For great art represents nature in such a way as to arouse in us the feeling that we possess a power which is not subject to nature's limitations, the power to think universal ideas and to formulate the unconditional moral law. This feeling is what Kant calls the beautiful and sublime, for it suggests that there is a final purpose in the universe: rational man legislating and obeying the law in a world which is otherwise meaningless. Art, if it attains to this goal, is the extension of ethics. Just as the categorical imperative commands that we act "as if" the maxim of our action were to become, through our will, "a universal law of nature," the great artist regards nature "as if" it worked in the direction of the final purpose of the world—man as an end in himself. Artistic genius is a talent which functions like nature in that it creates with a purpose in the same way that nature does disinterestedly and without design. As a sort of re-creation of nature, genius shows that the world of nature and freedom are not altogether separate, but have some kind of common basis. This creativity is what Kant meant in saying that the antithesis between nature and culture will be overcome only when art becomes strong enough to become "second nature. This is the ultimate moral end of the human species" (*Conjectural Beginning*).

Kant and Rousseau

From all this it is clear how Rousseau could exercise such a great influence on Kant. Both considered the moral law to be a matter of self-determination, yet at the same time the law of all rational beings. Both considered the fulfillment of the moral law to be man's only serious task, a task which defines and brings into being human nature proper. Both looked upon absolute freedom as the indispensable condition to this end. Both looked upon the loss of nature as irrevocable and on the conflict between nature and culture as the basic source of human misery. Both advocated republican government as a necessary step in the realization of the moral law. Finally, both visualized the eventual overcoming of the disunity in man and society by the fusion of theory and practice.

But, for all their agreement, there are significant differences between Kant and Rousseau. Kant did not proceed from a hypothetical construction of the state of nature and the transition from it to civil society. He abandoned the whole procedure of combatting the established order in the name of an improvised idealization of nature. He rightly rejected a method that depended on inventions about the distant past, and confined himself to empirically ascertainable facts. For Kant, civilization was not something superimposed on man, a contingency of human nature, but rather its very essence. In this respect, he marked a real advance over Rousseau. But the fact that he only reversed the value of the terms of the problem of civilization, without really abandoning them, is indicative of the extent to which Kant himself still belonged to the Enlightenment. Instead of setting an idealized conception of nature over against a corrupt society, he postulated an original, a priori "conflict of the natural and the moral species." In his view, man's ethical development takes place in almost inverse proportion to the empirical satisfaction of the individual. There is little room in Kant's philosophy for the realization of happiness; at best man can only make himself "worthy of happiness." He would have considered as irrelevant Rousseau's assertion of "the sweet feeling of existence independent of any other sensation." The value of existence, for Kant, did not depend at all on what happens to a person, but exclusively on what a person does. For him, there was no middle term between man as a natural and as a moral being; the fulfillment of man, therefore, did not lie in their reconciliation, but rather in the complete overcoming of nature (and history) by an abstract moral man.

Rousseau, on the other hand, would have insisted that what happens to a person, what is inflicted on him from without, and what a person does of his own volition are equally relevant because they are interdependent. Both are undeniable facts of life. And, for him, there does exist a middle term between natural and moral man. It consists precisely in this interaction between man and the world which is the substance of history and which finds expression in man's legitimate will to survival and happiness. Unlike Kant, Rousseau could never conceive true virtue apart from true happiness. One depends on the other, neither can thrive without the other, and both are without value in disjunction. Virtue, for him, is not an abstract imperative but a vital existential one. Hence, there is only one human nature, in his view, not two, as for Kant: one natural and one moral. If conflict rather than harmony prevails in the human world, this is due to the corrupt development of society, not to an original antithesis in human nature. Discord among men, and within the individual, is the result of history, not its cause. In the *Discourse on Inequality*, he "proves" that moral corruption "is not by any means the original state of man, but that it is merely the spirit of society, and the inequality that society produces, that thus transform and alter all our natural inclinations." For Rousseau, the healing of man can only come through a healing of society; for Kant, the healing of society will result only from a healing of the isolated, individual spirit.

THE
ENLIGHTENMENT
IN GERMANY

Germany in the Eighteenth Century

The Enlightenment reached its limits in France once it became the adequate ideological expression of the interests of the bourgeoisie, the strongest and most progressive class in that country. Rousseau himself, who overstepped these limits by espousing a radically democratic and egalitarian social doctrine, exerted little influence before the last quarter of the century, when the lower orders of the Third Estate began to stir. In politically fragmented Germany, which was hopelessly backward socially and economically compared to England and France, the middle class was weak and subservient, and a progressive intellectual tradition was scarcely compatible with the interests of the overwhelmingly dominant nobility. The German intelligentsia quite naturally adapted itself, either by choice or by necessity, to a society in which its ideas could find little or no support. There was no German national state with which all Germans could identify. The Holy Roman Empire, which, Voltaire correctly observed, was neither holy, nor Roman, nor an empire, was a ghost of its former self and long since surpassed by the modern nation-state.

There was no national past to give Germans a sense of collective existence and destiny, and which German writers might draw on for subject matter, thus linking themselves with the German people as a whole. There was no thriving capitalist economy and consequently no self-respecting, cosmopolitan middle class, whose existence might have made German thinkers more susceptible to progressive bourgeois values and a materialistic outlook. There was no great national center of cultural and intellectual ferment in Germany comparable to Paris and London. Such activity was confined mainly to small, stifling, oasislike university towns, like Göttingen, and occasional petty courts like Weimar. Many English and French writers in the eighteenth century were able to earn an independent livelihood, and a few, like Voltaire, even managed to amass fortunes from their writing. German writers were still dependent on patronage and university appointments; and if they declined or were denied these, they were forced to eke out miserable existences as tutors or clergymen. Lessing, the first German writer of importance to seek both intellectual and financial independence as a writer, paid a stiff price for this aspiration; he died an impoverished librarian at Wolfenbüttel.

It was this general abjectness of German society and the adaptation of the intelligentsia to it that gave the German Enlightenment its distinctive character. German thinkers tended to see a sharp opposition between the world of thought and social reality, and between an ideal past (whether Greek or medieval) and a dismal present. They tended to substitute the ideal of inner freedom for political freedom, to advocate the sovereignty of the spirit over empirical reality, and to predicate the reform of society on cultural reform. Romanticism, as one form or another of flight from the present world, found its homeland in Germany. All these tendencies amounted to an elaborate, and sometimes amazingly pedantic and obtuse, rationalization of the very real semifeudal political and social conditions out of which they grew. At the same time, however, the fact that ideas posed no threat to this society was conducive to the philosophical and literary exploration of new avenues of approach to the world and to the adaptation of the Enlightenment in Germany along highly original lines.

Kant exemplifies very well the peculiar character of the German Enlightenment. On the one hand, as we have seen, he fully subscribed to the progressive ideals of the French Enlightenment. On the other, he tended to view them as "ideas" in juxtaposition to and more real than the empirical world. From his vantage point of East Prussia, a caricature of enlightened government under the cynical rule of Frederick the Great,* there seemed little prospect for the realization of these ideals, unless they were sharply separated from the mechanistic and inhuman empirical world and made its driving force. So sharp was his distinction between appearance and reality, however, that reality ceased even to be knowable; one could only act "as if" it existed at all. So radical was Kant's dualism that, paradoxically, his effort to save human freedom and dignity seemed to result in a new form of philosophical fatalism. For if

---

* Lessing, who was in a very good position to know, called the Prussia of Frederick "the most slavish land in Europe"; and the so-called "Berlin freedom," much vaunted by later nationalistic German historians, he dubbed "the freedom to hawk as many anti-religious imbecilities as one wishes." But nothing is more indicative of Frederick's rule than a remark he makes himself in his *Histoire de mon Temps*: "I trust posterity will do me justice and understand how to distinguish the king in me from the philosopher, the decent from the political man."

reality determines all human behavior, yet cannot be known, how can they be freely chosen and translated into actuality? Conversely, if man as a phenomenon is strictly subject to the law of causality, what possible motive could he have for acting in accordance with the moral law? And, even if he wished, how could he do so? In a word, what was to be gained by replacing a materialist metaphysics with an idealist metaphysics? The great nineteenth-century German Jewish poet, Heinrich Heine, aptly stated the dilemma of Kantian philosophy thus: "It is a fearful thing when the bodies we have created demand of us a soul; but it is a far more dreadful, more terrible, more awful thing when we have created a soul, to hear that soul demanding of us a body, and to behold it pursuing us with this demand." This dilemma, which is not unusual in the history of German thought, amply attests how infertile German soil was for the growth of humanism. Nevertheless, Kant opened up a whole new approach to an understanding of the relationship between subject and object, and between theory and practice which came to fruition later in Hegel's philosophy of dialectic. Kantian philosophy, in its combination of idealistic illusion and methodological originalty, is typical of the German Enlightenment.

Goethe: Naturalism and Humanism

Kant's revolt against nature, which had its roots in Rousseau, formed one pole of the German Enlightenment. The other, a new humanistic conception of nature, which was also inspired in part by Rousseau, found its highest expression in Johann Wolfgang von Goethe (1749–1832), whose first novel, *The Sorrows of Young Werther* (1774), marked the passing of artistic and intellectual hegemony from France to Germany. The high artistic quality of this tragic love story, Germany's first contribution to world letters, and the fact that it became immediately popular everywhere (Werther's costume even became the fashion for a time) indicates how sensitive international society was by now to its theme: the conflict of the individual within himself and with society at large. At the very center of *Werther* is the problem of humanism and the possibility of its realization in the modern world. Werther, the heroic protagonist of the ideal of full and harmonious development of the human personality, comes into conflict not only with a pompous and decadent aristocracy, but also with a stagnant and philistine bourgeoisie as represented by Albert, the fiancé of his beloved Lotte. Hence, when Goethe appeals to nature in this novel, it is no longer nature conceived in the image of the middle class with its ideology of mechanistic rationalism. Rather it is a nature enlivened and set over against aristocracy and bourgeoisie alike. Nature is seen now as the source of human spontaneity and inventiveness; art itself is nothing more than the fulfillment of nature in the fully formed personality. "Nature alone is infinitely rich, and she alone favors the great artist. One can say much in favor of rules, about the same thing that can be said in praise of civil society. . . . On the other hand, any 'rule,' say what you like, will destroy the true feeling for nature and the true expression of her." This conception of nature as a new human ideal was fundamental to Goethe's whole creative life. Much later, in his *Dichtung und Wahrheit*, he restated it thus: "Whatever a man strives to achieve . . . must arise from the totality of his unified powers; everything isolated is harmful."

Goethe's "Werther"

In contrast to Kant, Goethe denied that the discord in the human world stemmed from a conflict between ignoble and egoistic natural impulses, on the one hand, and noble ethical maxims on the other; that is, from an a priori "conflict between the natural and the moral species." On the contrary, the tragedy of Werther, his *Weltschmerz*, his disgust with the world, arise from the fact that his passions are lofty and fine, but are thwarted by the world in which he lives. His fate served to illustrate Goethe's own very un-Kantian view that the law is made for the sake of man, not man for the sake of the law. In his younger years, before he became disillusioned with the French Revolution, Goethe would have agreed with the view of his friend at that time, Friedrich Jacobi (1743–1819), that rebellion is "the majestic right of man, the mark of his dignity." To Albert's statement that "certain actions remain morally wrong, no matter what their motivations may be," Werther answers: "It is true that theft is wrong; but does the man who sets out to steal in order to save himself and his family from imminent starvation deserve sympathy or punishment? . . . Even our very laws, coldblooded pedants that they are, let themselves be moved and withhold their penalties." Werther's finest thoughts are just those that spring from his feelings. The high moral value Goethe attributed to feeling is evident in Werther's remark: "It is surely a fact that nothing in the world but love makes a person indispensable." Goethe notes again the interrelationship of natural and moral man in his description of Werther's disintegration: "The intimidation of his heart consumed all the forces of his mind, his vivacity and his perceptions; he became a sad figure in society, steadily more unhappy, and his injustice to others grew with his own unhappiness." Finally, Werther's suicide, like that of Montesquieu's Roxane and Lessing's Emilia Galotti, was a humanist protest against the frustration of nature by a corrupt society.

If Kant drew inspiration from Rousseau's rational theory of the general will, the young Goethe represents a continuation of Rousseau the man of sensibility. As with Rousseau, Werther's struggle for the realization of his personality finds expression in his identification with the lower classes. Although an image of the middle-class Goethe himself, Werther observes that the human qualities he admires most are to be found in "complete genuineness . . . amid that class of people whom we call uncultured, whom we call crude. We refined ones—refined until there is nothing left." He remarks that "he who thinks it necessary to withdraw from the so-called rabble in order to keep their respect is just as reprehensible as a coward who hides from his enemy because he is afraid of defeat." The authors whom Werther admires—Homer, Ossian, Goldsmith, and Lessing—are great in his eyes because they are popular writers. After he is snubbed by the aristocrats at the legation where he reluctantly accepted employment, Werther wanders off alone to read "the fine canto in which Ulysses enjoys the hospitality of the excellent swineherd. All that was good." Even his defense of suicide against the philistine Albert has a social revolutionary overtone: "If a nation is sighing under the unendurable yoke of a tyrant, do you dare speak of weakness if the people rise up in rage and rend their fetters?"

The tension between Werther and the world comes to a head in his relationship with Lotte, who finds herself caught between her love for him, which she strives to deny, and the obligation she feels toward her marriage to Albert. Her decision to remain true to her husband is what precipitates Werther's suicide. But the love theme is so persuasive precisely because it encompasses all the essential elements of the social world in which it unfolds. Lotte, a bourgeois herself, cannot bring herself to violate the "rule" of marriage for the sake of real love, nor to sacrifice security to poetry. She fears a man who thinks that, "Everything in the world comes down to mere trumpery, and one who wears himself out because others want him to, without gratifying his own passion or satisfying his own needs, but seeking money, or prestige, or whatever, is bound to be a fool." Yet, she loves him, and in renouncing this love, she brings unhappiness on herself, *not* moral fulfillment: ". . . it was her secret, heartfelt desire to keep him for herself, and she was saying to herself the while that she could not keep him, might not keep him; her pure, fine, generally lighthearted spirit, so ready to help itself, felt the burden of a melancholy which knows that the prospect of happiness is sealed off." Politically, young Goethe was no revolutionary, and certainly not a socialist. Yet, in setting his ideal of the fully formed personality against the sterility and exclusionism of the upper classes, on the one hand, and against the philistinism of the bourgeoisie on the other, he found himself viewing with sympathy and admiration the victims of this environment. Werther was borne to his grave by workmen; no one else was present, not even a clergyman.

Goethe's "Wilhelm Meister"

Goethe expanded this theme in *Wilhelm Meister's Apprenticeship*, a novel begun in the seventies but not completed until 1796. Instead of resolving the conflict between the hero and society by suicide, as a passionate protest against the dehumanization of man, Goethe raises the question here of what forms of insight and what strengths of character are necessary to preserve the humanist ideal within a constricting and degraded social order. The series of encounters, relationships, and symbolic episodes which Meister undergoes comprise his "apprenticeship," a long and difficult process of growth and self-definition which enables him in the end to relate to the world without being destroyed by it yet without compromising himself. This gradual process of *Bildung* or self-education Goethe conceived as a sort of artistic experience in which "infinitely rich" nature is brought to perfection in human life in the form of human inventiveness. In fact, the well-lived life *is* a work of art, and the problem of art is no less than the problem of life itself. Goethe defines genius, for example, as only the normal man fully developed. Hence his predilection for conceiving the hero as artist (*e.g.*, Tasso and Meister himself). This interpenetration of art and life is evident in Meister's remark that the poet is able to rise above the turmoil of the world only because he has "a fellow-feeling of the mournful and joyful in the fate of all human beings . . ." Most men suffer "continual discontent and agitation" because they "cannot make realities correspond to their conceptions." The poet, who has this fellow-feeling lacking in others, is able to do so; this is what distinguishes him from the rest of mankind.

Wilhelm Meister, rather than being a departure from the Enlightenment, is its literary culmination. Enlightenment is life itself here, and Goethe's conception of the good life as education and art represents the pinnacle of human freedom as defined, for example, by Voltaire: "Liberty . . . is, when accurately defined, only the power of acting." This theme is reiterated constantly in *Meister*: "For man . . . there is but one misfortune; when some idea lays hold of him, which exerts no influence upon active life, or still more, which withdraws him from it." Madness even is explained as a result of the frustration of the power to act. The wise physician remarks: "The means of curing madness seem to me extremely simple. They are the very means by which you hinder sane persons from becoming mad. Awaken their activity; accustom them to order; bring them to perceive that they hold their being and fate in common with many millions. . . . Doubt of any kind can be removed by nothing but activity. Nothing more exposes us to madness than distinguishing ourselves from others, and nothing contributes more to maintaining our common sense than living in the universal way with multitudes of men. Alas! how much there is in education and in our institutions to prepare us and our children for insanity!" The moral of *Meister* is the education of men for the practical understanding of reality, with the aim of bringing them to self-fulfillment in a spirit and in an atmosphere of spontaneity and sociability.

Man and the world are related in *Meister* by Goethe's passionate faith in the capacity of the spirit to harmonize the interplay between resoluteness and fate, between reason and feeling, and between the individual and society. This faith is the standard by which he judges the vast array of characters and classes portrayed in this novel. The chief obstacle to Meister's growth toward self-definition, and what makes it such a pressing problem in the first place, is the incompatibility of his personal ideal and the degraded condition of German society. Like Werther, Meister castigates the nobility, who have the material means to achieve a high level of human culture, but who rarely do so.

> The man for whom inherited wealth has secured a perfect freedom of existence; who finds himself from his youth on abundantly surrounded by all the secondary essentials, so to speak, of human life, will generally become accustomed to considering these qualifications as the first and foremost; while the worth of that mode of human life, which nature from her own stores equips and furnishes, will strike him much more faintly. The behavior of noblemen to their inferiors, and likewise to each other, is regulated by externalities: they give each other credit for his title, his rank, his clothes, and equipage, but his individual merits do not come into play.

On the other hand, in a letter to his boyhood friend Werner, the Albert in this novel, Meister also berates the bourgeois class into which he was born.

> The burgher may not ask himself, 'What are you?' He can only ask, 'What have you? What discernment, knowledge, talent, wealth?' . . . He must cultivate some single gift in order to be useful, and it is beforehand settled, that in his way of life there is no harmony, and can be none, since he is bound to make himself of use in one department, and so has to relinquish all the others. . . . My present business is to meet my own case, as matters actually stand; to consider by what means I may save myself, and reach the object which I cannot live in peace without. Now this harmonious cultivation of my nature,

which has been denied me by birth, is exactly what I most long for.

It is no accident that *Meister* was written in the form of an educational novel (*Bildungsroman*), a genre of which it is the finest example. In a society which offered no human models worthy of imitation, no common history or culture for writers to draw on; a society which hindered the individual every step of the way in his quest for human perfection, what choice did a person have but to pick his way slowly and painfully toward it, dependent only on himself and on his own resources? *Meister* was intended to provide a human model for such a society. With regard to literary forms, Wilhelm, speaking for Goethe himself, observes that "Fate, which by means of outward unconnected circumstances, carries men forward, without their own concurrence, to an unforeseen catastrophe, can have a place only in the drama"; whereas the novel allows for chance which "may produce pathetic situations, but never tragic ones." Goethe's choice of the form of the novel in this instance stemmed from a desire to instil in the reader a will to resist Fate by means of *Bildung*.

Thus, hatred of Fate is preached throughout the novel, and *Meister* turns out to be an implicit polemic against the metaphysical fatalism of Kant's moral philosophy. "He alone is worthy of respect who knows what is of use to himself and others, and who labors to control his self-will." The educators in *Meister,* Jarno and the abbé, Lothario and Nathalie, who embody the characteristic Enlightenment faith in man's ability to create a life of compassion, tolerance, and purposeful activity, reject "imperatives" of any sort. Instead of man making himself servile to any law, moral or otherwise, he is urged to become sociable through experience and self-determination, bringing his personality into harmony with the happiness and human interests of his fellowmen. Goethe believed that the ideals of humanism are rooted in the depths of human nature itself. *Bildung* is the process by which man is able to bring his latent humanity to fruition. But the very social conditions which gave rise to this German version of enlightenment are the same which thwarted its realization. Thus, while Meister finds self-fulfillment in the end, Goethe realistically allows this to happen only within the confines of an exclusive humanist utopia made up of an unrepresentative handful of enlightened aristocrats and bourgeois who, in the interest of self-preservation, set themselves off from society at large. As a realist, Goethe could not close his novel on a bright note in any other way. This utopian impasse in which *Meister* ends suggests why it represents the transition in literature from the Enlightenment to nineteenth-century social realism.

Genesis of German Humanism: Leibniz

These ideas, which found their supreme literary expression in Goethe, were not new with him, however, nor were they solely a continuation of Rosseau's thought. Goethe also drew on a native German philosophical tradition which went back to Gottfried Wilhelm Leibniz (1646–1716) and through him, to Renaissance neo-Platonism—a tradition carried forward in Germany after Leibniz by Gotthold Ephraim Lessing (1729–1781) and Johann Gottfried Herder (1744–1803). Leibniz sought to develop a theory which would explain the coexistence of both unity and multiplicity in nature, constancy and change, and the apparent harmony between mind and matter. The result was his theory of monads which, like the atomic theory, undertook to define the basic stuff of the universe and to show how the complex universe is formed out of it. Leibniz visualized the monad as a sort of microcosm of the universe, characterized by the same dynamism and self-sufficiency characteristic of nature as a whole. His monads, like Newton's atoms, are simple, indivisible, and imperishable. However, unlike atoms, which are uniform, inert, and material, Leibniz's monads are each a unique and self-developing vital field of force. Whereas the atom is acted on from without, the monad is "windowless," completely self-determining—Leibniz's view being that anything subject to external causation cannot be called basic reality. The sum of monads, all acting in unison according to a preestablished cosmic harmony, constitute the whole of the universe.

This theory clearly shows a shift in emphasis from a mechanistic to an organic view of nature. Each monad possesses some degree of consciousness and is engaged in a ceaseless process of self-activation. In a state of constant activity, it develops and strives for self-realization through a series of acts of individuation. And, since it is wholly self-contained, the monad preserves its past and contains its future throughout its transitions from one state to the next. Its unity is that of continuity and coherence, rather than that of simple correspondence. (A man at forty obviously does not resemble what he was as an infant, yet he preserves an identity he had as an infant throughout the changes brought by growth.) The principle of continuity enables us to distinguish being in becoming, constancy in change, unity in multiplicity—terms which are not antithetical in the monad but reciprocal and correlated. The whole of a thing is greater than the sum of its parts and is presupposed by them as an a priori condition of their existence and particular configuration. This can be seen in the life of the soul, which is the prime example of a monad. In Leibniz's view, our present state of mind is continuous with, and can only be explained by, our previous states of mind, all of which in turn foreshadow its future states.

It is clear how Leibniz's stress on the self-determination and evolutionary coherence of the monad could pave the way for Goethe's conception of *Bildung*. The development of the monad is literally a self-unfolding, a process of maturation and self-definition. This process involves bringing to fruition contents which existed at the outset, but in an obscure and latent form. Leibniz was concerned to avoid the attitude of resignation in the face of determinant external forces which he believed was implicit in the philosophies of Descartes, Spinoza, and Locke. Thus, he offered a theory emphasizing the free effort of each person to attain clearness and the realization of his own individual nature. Everything in the intellect is first in the senses, Leibniz agreed with Locke—"except the intellect itself." However, as his theory did not allow for the differences between monads to be explained by differences in the environment, or to differences in their position within it, he accounted for the individuality of the monads by the difference in their development between the two poles of darkness and distinctness. These two poles are separated by a wide range of gradations which the monad traverses in the course of its self-actuation. Since the human monad, like all monads, is self-enclosed, the disappearance of content from the mind is only apparent; in reality it simply lapses into a darker, more unconscious state than when it was first experienced (a view that obviously anticipates depth psychology). Leibniz attributed evil to this lack of clarity or actuation, rather than to deliberate acts of the will or to the existence of forces antithetical to the forces of good. Like Plato, he equated goodness with reality and evil with its absence. The existence of evil is explained as an inevitable imperfection of creatures who, because they are finite, can never attain to complete fullness of being. This is the best of all possible worlds, but at best it is still imperfect. Nonetheless, within this limitation there is a broad scope for self-perfection. By an act of free will anyone may elect to strive toward it. In proportion as he succeeds, he finds his own happiness. And, in the process, he necessarily contributes to the happiness of others. For we love in others what we seek for ourselves. This disinterested love, which few achieve, though it combines the good *and* the desirable, is the sign of the attainment of reality in and through ethical perfection.

Lessing

Lessing incorporated many of Leibniz's ideas in his thinking on religion and aesthetics. His *Education of the Human Race* (1781) attempts to show that religion is a divine plan for the education of man through history. The various religions basically do not conflict; they are all equally valid as phases in the unfolding of the eternal in time. The whole worth of religion lies precisely in the dignity which accrues to the human spirit as it seeks to grasp the universal amid the temporal flux. For Lessing, the worth of man does not consist in the possession of truth, which makes him "quiescent, indolent, proud," but rather in his striving for it. For it is this striving for truth which enlarges man's powers of understanding. "Not the truth which is at the disposal of every man, but the honest pains he has taken to come by the truth make the worth of a man. For not through the possession, but through the pursuit of truth, do his powers increase, and in this alone consists his ever increasing perfection." This heterodox view, that no religion possesses absolute truth, but that each is equally valid in mankind's progress toward truth, Lessing dramatized in his last and best known play, *Nathan the Wise* (1779).

Rather than saving religion, however, Lessing transformed the religious question into a historical one. The real importance of his views on religion, the field in which the Enlightenment fought most of its major intellectual battles, is that they paved the way for a deeper and more dedicated understanding of historical reality. Lessing came to regard history as the medium through which reason gradually comes to fruition. In this respect, he anticipated Kant. Both saw in history infinite reason manifesting itself in the finite. Unlike Kant, however, Lessing tended toward Spinozistic monism or pantheism. In agreement with Spinoza, whom he greatly admired, Lessing declined to believe in a personal God which, he claimed, would require an irrational leap of faith too much to ask of his "old legs and heavy head." Instead, he took the position of this seventeenth-century Jewish heretic that God is the soul of the universe, indistinguishable from the universe, and meaningless if conceived apart from it. (Lessing contributed to the revival of three great figures hitherto passed over by the Enlightenment: Aristotle, Shakespeare, and Spinoza). This view imparted to Lessing's view of history a high seriousness always lacking in that of Kant. Also un-Kantian was his agreement with Leibniz's conceptions of continuity and the polarity of darkness and distinctness. Lessing, like Leibniz, regarded feeling as basically a dark and undeveloped idea, but still an idea; so that reason and feeling were rarely disassociated in his mind. By preserving their unity in this way, he upheld and reinvigorated the humanistic core of the Enlightenment. But, whereas the new status ascribed to feeling by Rousseau manifested itself in political and social ferment in France, in Germany it contributed to philosophical and artistic ferment and an overriding concern with history and psychology. There the illusion developed that political and social evils could be exorcised by a healing, as it were, of man's philosophical, artistic, or historical consciousness.

Lessing, for example, believed that a reformed theater would help prepare Germans for enlightened nationhood; an idea followed up by Herder, Goethe, and Schiller. His *Hamburg Dramaturgy* (1767–1769) called for the restoration in modern drama of the true Aristotelian idea of tragedy. According to Aristotle, it is not primarily subject matter that defines tragedy, but rather the impact of fear and pity that a drama produces on the audience. Lessing claimed in this writing that the great French tragedians, Corneille in particular, adhered only superficially to Aristotle's principles of tragedy. They aimed more at arousing admiration than fear or pity, thus reducing tragic drama to a courtly function, to an ideological support of the court aristocracy. Lessing's concern with the seemingly remote problem of the true principles of tragedy and his criticism of the leading French tragedians (whom he greatly admired, though he thought they were not *tragedians*), arose out of his dislike of aristocratic attitudes and the pernicious effect that their glorification in French drama had in Germany, where the upper classes aped French modes and where the arts served to support the social predominance of the aristocracy. (Frederick the Great was typical of his class in that he spoke and wrote in French, considering German a barbarous language.) Thus, the reform of German theater along Aristotelian lines was associated in Lessing's mind with the enlightened aim of undercutting the aristocracy whose position in the social hierarchy was strengthened by the acceptance in Germany of French literary styles.

Lessing stressed the unity in tragedy between character and destiny. The fate of a tragic figure must follow necessarily from his or her character. This, he claimed, was the essence of Aristotle's unity of action—a principle understood correctly not by Corneille but by Shakespeare, whom Lessing regarded as *the* great modern tragedian. By his ability to effect this unity of action, Shakespeare attained to genius, a term defined by Lessing thus:

> Genius is concerned only with events that are rooted in one another, that form a chain of cause and effect. To reduce the latter to the former, to weigh the latter against the former, everywhere to exclude chance, to cause everything that occurs to occur so that it could not have happened otherwise—this is the role of genius when it deals with matters of history and converts the useless treasures of memory into nourishment for the soul. (*Hamburg Dramaturgy.*)

Genius, for Lessing, far from being irrational, is the very epitome of reason. The world which it creates is based on the unity of cause and effect and on the complete exclusion of chance.

By exposing the aristocratic ideology underlying French drama, Lessing hoped to pave the way for the writing of middle-class tragedies in Germany. His own middle-class tragedy, *Emilia Galotti* (1772), was intended to illustrate his dramatic theory. Strangely enough, however, this drama fails as a tragedy precisely because Lessing, in depicting his bourgeois heroine, failed to achieve the unity between character and destiny which he so vigorously advocated. The death of Emilia, who is presented as a simple, innocent girl with a religious sense, was supposed to be a moral indictment of the corrupt and irresponsible nobility of the petty German courts. The tragic climax of the play was supposed to result from an inexorable necessity derived from the very nature of the character involved. The crisis of the final scene when Odoardo, the father, stabs his beloved daughter, does not seem to follow from Emilia's character, nor to be justified by it.

Lessing himself observed that middle-class life in Germany was too narrow and impoverished to lend itself easily to tragic treatment, that it was in fact a fit subject only for comedy. His finest play, and the only one set in Germany, was a comedy, *Minna von Barnhelm* (1767). Just as Lessing chose a foreign setting for his first tragedy, *Miss Sara Sampson* (1755), in order to endow his middle-class characters with a dignity lacking in the German middle class, he felt it necessary to do the same with *Emilia Galotti*. The reason for the dramatic failure of this tragedy lies less in Emilia's character than in the narrowness of the German middle-class life whose values she shares. Lessing seems to have felt that, in order to make this play a tragedy, he either had to falsify social reality of else compromise his dramatic principles. He chose the latter course. The tragedy of *Emilia Galotti* is not that of Emilia, but the tragedy of Lessing, and of the German Enlightenment as a whole.

Political particularism was one important reason why a popular national theater was impossible in Germany. The individual states, often no larger than estates, were too small and insulated to inspire a sense of social solidarity and responsibility. Even the Hamburg National Theater, for which the sponsors had high hopes, and which occasioned Lessing's *Hamburg Dramaturgy*, folded less than a year after its opening. Since German writers could not find inspiration in German national life, they continued either to imitate foreign models, or else succeeded in developing an artistic originality which came in advance of and substituted for political patriotism. Goethe, who in his later years was forever comparing Germany unfavorably to France in this respect, and who admired the high level of general culture in France, summed up the ill effect of Germany's political condition on German literature in his essay, *Literarische Sansculottismus* (1795). A classical "national author" can only appear, he says, "if the history of his nation furnishes him with a happy and significant series of great events and their consequences; if his fellow countrymen show him examples of high thinking, deep feeling, and bold, sustained action; if he himself, filled with this spirit of his nation, feels he has genius enough within him to share sympathetically both its past and present life."

The political disunity of Germany, however, was only one aspect of its general degradation, and not the most important one in the eyes of the Storm and Stress writers of the seventies and eighties. In their youth, Herder, Goethe, and Schiller, Lenz, Iffland and Klinger were animated more by class consciousness than by nationalism. Influenced by the writers of social protest in France, particularly Diderot and Rousseau, they usually devoted their talents to dramatizing the class antagonisms in Germany and almost always sided with the middle class. It was the contempt these writers, like Lessing, had for the "Gallomania" (Schiller) of the German aristocracy (a contempt Tolstoy felt toward the Russian aristocracy a century later) that motivated their hostility to French art forms; although this hostility was inspired, paradoxically, by French critics themselves. It was Schiller, the writer of social protest, that the French National Assembly made a "citoyen" of the Republic.

Schiller

Nevertheless, the social realism of the Storm and Stress writers was largely superficial. Bourgeois themselves, they portrayed their class as unhappy but virtuous, and the nobility as corrupt and vicious. The characteristic defects of the German middle class, its philistinism, servility, and cloying sentimentalism, they attributed to unfavorable social conditions. Yet, their plays were themselves too narrow in scope to include the broad social and political realities which were responsible for the situation. Hence, they could evoke little more than an emotional response. Even the boldest of the Storm and Stress dramas, Schiller's *Love and Intrigue* (1783), conveys no comprehensive grasp of social reality.

What Erich Auerbach says of the early Schiller might well apply in fact to the Storm and Stress movement as a whole: "Schiller knew much more *against* what than *for* what he was fighting. . . . We hear and sense practically nothing [in *Love and Intrigue*] of inner problems, historical complications, the function of the ruling class, the causes of its moral decline, nor of practical conditions in the principality. This is not realism, it is melodrama." This artistic failing, however, and the general failure of Storm and Stress as a literary movement, are due in the last analysis to the degradation of the middle class itself, which made it difficult for these writers to know what they were fighting *for*. The absence of a revolutionary political consciousness in society at large hindered them from developing an ideological viewpoint broad enough and progressive enough to enable them to analyze the social evils they condemned and to propose an effective solution to them. Consequently, the theater could serve only as "a kind of substitute for the pulpit" (Bruford). Storm and Stress, like the similar movement of German Expressionism in the twentieth-century, was short-lived; Herder and Goethe resigned themselves to their official functions at Weimar, and Klinger embarked on a successful career at the Russian court. Along with faith in enlightenment, we also find resignation reflected in eighteenth-century German literature.

Herder

This combination is also apparent in the emerging new sense of history, of which Herder was the best exemplar. Since there was no national history to speak of, German historical thought tended right from the beginning to develop in two diametrically opposite directions: extreme particularism and extreme universalism. Justus Möser (1720–1794), representative of the first, confined himself to the study of a single territory, his native Osnabrück; while Herder, representative of the second, took as his theme nothing less than the universe itself. Instead of political and military events, they emphasized culture, native folkways, and the workaday world, viewing them as the substance and dynamics of history. Voltaire and others in France and England had already used this approach in their own historical writings. But the Germans, who had little reason to be optimistic about the present, criticized the French for viewing the past merely as an error serving only to glorify the present. History, for Herder, was not primarily a way of explaining the present by the past, but rather a means of stimulating men to see themselves in relation to and as part of a great continuum embracing past, present, and future. This approach, which came to be known as historicism, sought to understand each past age in its own terms, as a necessary but transitory phase in this continuum. The practical function of history was to enable contemporary man to understand other men living at different times and under different conditions, struggling like himself, but with different means, to realize universally valid human values. This effort to induce the individual to consider his personal destiny in the light of the destiny of mankind as a whole is what was new and fruitful in Herder's historical conception.

During the seventies and eighties, Goethe learned from him that history is an uninterrupted succession of unique phases, each of which is indispensable to the total process, but each of which is valid in itself, having "its own core of happiness, just as any sphere has its own center of gravity." He learned from Herder that "all being alike is an indivisible idea; in the greatest as well as in the least, founded on the same laws." He learned that the life cycle of the individual is analogous to that of the whole human race and recapitulates it palingenetically—a conception which found its way into *Faust*. He also learned that the unity of history does not lie in the uniformity of its phases, but rather in its heterogeneity, in the fulness of being. In a letter to a friend, in which Goethe expressed his agreement with Herder's general historical conception, he writes: "And so every creature is only one note, one nuance of a greater harmony, which must be studied as a single process, or every individual remains a dead letter." The whole weight of the heroic side of the Enlightenment—the humanism of Montesquieu, Voltaire, Diderot, and Rousseau, of Leibniz, Lessing, Kant, and Herder—is evident in this statement.

Herder correctly believed that an awakening of the

national consciousness of Germans was a necessary condition for political unification. But since conditions in Germany precluded political and social reform, he, like most of his contemporaries, appealed to spiritual and cultural regeneration. In making culture the ground of national unification in this situation, he tended to view it as a natural, organically necessary growth, distinct from and even opposed to the political and social environment in which it originates. As action was not possible in Germany, the best alternative seemed to be a theory of history according to which the past, by its own intrinsic momentum, would lead to a better future. Herder's writings abound in botanical imagery and analogies drawn from nature which suggest the inevitability of progress, but without any exertion on the part of the human agents involved. The transformation of society will occur, but in the mysterious manner of the metamorphosis of a plant. Whereas Rousseau opposed an ideal state of nature to history as a means to force history into a new direction, Herder tended to view history itself as the *natural* development of human nature. He continued to hold to the ideal of progress, but interpreted it as a sort of irrational inner necessity of the human spirit.

Herder typifies the tragedy of the German Enlightenment in that he faced a situation which he was neither willing to accept nor able to surmount. The result was an attitude of withdrawal and stoic resignation which pervades his theory of national regeneration. In his opposition to despotism and oppression, he envisaged the nation not as the embodiment of a common will, but rather of a common nature. The nation was not a citizenry defined by common political rights and duties, but rather a *Volk* defined by a common cultural heritage. Paradoxically, this founder of German nationalism "conceived the nation apart from and almost in opposition to the fatherland" (Carlo Antoni). In Herder we find the embryo of those false dichotomies between Culture and Civilization, and between Spirit and Life, which were voiced in one form or another by many later German thinkers, notably Schopenhauer, Burckhardt, Spengler, and Thomas Mann. German racist thinkers in the twentieth century simply carried Herder's views to their ugly, caricatural extreme when they advocated purging society of elements declared alien according to the criterion of culture conceived as a *natural* attribute.

SUMMARY AND CONCLUSION

The eighteenth century was the last and most vigorous phase in the transition from the medieval to the modern world. The frivolity, ennui, and foreboding of the unknown, which permeated the age from beginning to end, betokened an awareness of the fact that an old world was dissolving and a new world coming into being. It was the age of Swedenborg, Cagliostro, and Casanova as well as that of Montesquieu, Voltaire, and Rousseau; an age of mysticism, magic, and charlatanry as well as of enlightenment. But the transition was consummated when Renaissance humanism, the Reformation stress on the inner man, and seventeenth-century science and rational philosophy—movements which had hitherto coexisted relatively independent of one another —were fused by the enlighteners and forged into a revolutionary "religion of humanity."

The eighteenth century, says the contemporary theologian, Karl Barth, gave birth to absolute man. "Man, who discovers his own power and ability, the potentiality dormant in his humanity, that is, his human being as such, and looks upon it as the final, the real and absolute, I mean as something 'detached,' self-justifying, with its own authority and power, which he can therefore set in motion in all directions and without any restraint—this is absolute man." Despite the tone of disapproval, this characterization comes very close to expressing the essence of the Enlightenment. But the real

143

problem posed by the Enlightenment is not that it sanc-
tioned "absolute man," nor that it ended by rejecting all
external norms, whether providence or ultimately even
nature. For if "absolute man" has proved himself capable of
committing the worst crimes against humanity, it is also true,
according to Kingsley Martin, that the "religion of humanity
—the development of the individual within and through the
developing social organism—has, in spite of its misinterpre-
tations, inspired the most fruitful work which has been
done since the Revolution."

It may be that the Enlightenment resulted in the
alienation of modern man from a dead and indifferent nature; that we must now, according to modern science, regard
man "as little more than a chance deposit on the surface
of the world, carelessly thrown up between two ice ages by
the same forces that rust iron and ripen corn, a sentient
organism endowed by some happy or unhappy accident
with intelligence indeed, but with an intelligence that is
conditioned by the very forces that it seeks to understand
and to control" (C. Becker). It is not necessarily true, of
course, that a godless universe and a silent nature deprive
human life of meaning. It is only true that, in a meaningless
universe, men must bear the responsibility for giving value
to what they create and add to a world which they did not
make and which will outlive them. A consciousness of this
task is the lasting legacy of the Enlightenment.

The enlighteners knew the meaning of spiritual frustration, but they refused to accept the conclusion that it is
the inevitable and everlasting "human condition." They recognized that men long in vain to be gods, but they regarded
this longing as a sign of man's dignity and superlative aspiration, not as a cause for despair. If we no longer accept
these conclusions, it is not because the Enlightenment has

"failed" us, as so many, beginning with the Romantics, have maintained. If anything, the doleful pessimism so widespread in the modern world betokens its bad conscience at having failed the Enlightenment. The dead do not fail the living unless the living themselves allow this to happen.

The problem of the Enlightenment in relation to the modern world lies elsewhere—in the equation of the "religion of humanity" with private self-seeking, whether on the part of the individual, a nation, a class, or a race. If history since the French Revolution has "proved" anything, it is that this equation is a dangerous illusion. It is true that without it there would have been no Enlightenment and no French Revolution, for the enlighteners "found a society which had no informing principle of justice; in which there was no longer any relation between function and position; which was, in fact, nakedly a class domination even if its forces and its phraseology bore witness to a time when the aristocracy served as well as owned; and the Church taught as well as persecuted" (Martin). However, once the feudal hierarchy was overthrown by, and in the interest of, the one class which was in a position to perform this feat, there was nothing to prevent the victor from making use of this illusion to impose a new oppression—the oppression of the commercially powerful. And it is this new oppression, many will admit now, which has encouraged the mounting feeling that reason is sterile, that religious faith is necessary, that evil is inevitable, that life is tragic, and that despair is a "realistic" attitude. We have seen the seed of this development in the nascent polarization of the Enlightenment between the heroic and the bourgeois, between the ideal and the ideological, between the aspiration to liberty, equality, fraternity and the tendency toward fatalism—a seed which has long since blossomed into a glaring contradiction between a waning humanism and a triumphant bourgeois social order. The problem that the Enlightenment poses to our world is whether and how the ideal of progress toward human perfection, within and for the sake of a happier, freer, and more equal society, can survive this contradiction and come to fruition.

SELECTED BIBLIOGRAPHY

This brief annotated bibliography is intended to reflect works in English which significantly contributed to the preparation of this essay and to guide the interested college student and general reader.

GENERAL WORKS ON EIGHTEENTH-CENTURY EUROPE

Readers interested in furthering their understanding of the Enlightenment might best begin by enlarging their view of the broad sweep of eighteenth-century European history. The following books serve this purpose.

ANDERSON, M. S. *Europe in the Eighteenth Century, 1713–1789.* New York: Oxford Galaxy, 1966. The best one-volume survey in English, particularly good on Eastern Europe, on political developments and institutions in general, and on the importance of local variations and peculiarities of the European social structure.

WHITE, R. J. *Europe in the Eighteenth Century.* New York: St. Martin's, 1965. A thoughtful, well-written, balanced general survey.

New Cambridge Modern History, vol. VII: *The Old Regime, 1713–1763,* ed. J. O. Lindsay (Cambridge, Eng., 1957) and vol. VIII, *The American and French Revolutions, 1763–1793,* ed. by Albert Goodwin (Cambridge, Eng., 1965). Comprehensive and useful as reference works, but uneven in quality and lacking in coherence and continuity.

The following four surveys form part of the *Rise of Modern Europe* series, edited by William L. Langer. Although originally published in the 1940s, these works are still very useful and contain extensive bibliographies, which have been updated in the republished Harper Torchbook edition of the series.

WOLF, JOHN B. *The Emergence of the Great Powers, 1685–1715.* New York: Harper & Row, 1963.

ROBERTS, PENFIELD. *The Quest for Security, 1715–1740.* New York: Harper & Row, 1963.

DORN, WALTER L. *Competition for Empire, 1740–1763.* New York: Harper & Row, 1963.

GERSHOY, LEO. *From Despotism to Revolution, 1763–1789.* New York: Harper & Row, 1963.

As there are many easily available national histories in English for the eighteenth century, at least for the Western European countries, only a few of the best need be mentioned here.

COBBAN, ALFRED. *A History of Modern France,* vol. I: *1715–1799.* Harmondsworth: Penguin, 1957.

HOLBORN, HAJO. *A History of Modern Germany, 1648–1840.* New York: Knopf, 1968.

PLUMB, J. H. *England in the Eighteenth Century, 1714–1815.* Harmondsworth: Penguin, 1951.

POLITICS

The following works deal with important political events, institutions, and personalities of the period.

CRANKSHAW, EDWARD. *Maria Theresa.* New York: Viking, 1970. One of the few studies in English of this remarkable empress.

FAŸ, BERNARD. *Louis XVI: The End of a World.* Trans. by P. O'Brian. Chicago: H. Regnery, 1968. Examines the weaknesses of this monarch and his regime.

GAGLIARDO, JOHN G. *Enlightened Despotism.* New York: Crowell, 1967. A good recent essay on the reform movement designed to strengthen political absolutism.

GOOCH, GEORGE P. *Louis XV: Monarchy in Decline.* London: Longmans, Green, 1956. A standard work by one of Britain's most distinguished historians.

HARRIS, RONALD W. *Absolutism and Enlightenment, 1660–1789.* New York: Harper & Row, 1964. Better on absolutism than on enlightenment.

KRIEGER, LEONARD. *Kings and Philosophers, 1689–1789.* New York: Norton, 1970. A searching analysis of the relationship between political theory and practice during this century.

NAMIER, LEWIS B. *The Structure of Politics at the Accession of George III,* 2nd ed. New York: St. Martin's, 1957.

————. *England in the Age of the American Revolution,* 2nd ed. New York: St. Martin's, 1961. Two pioneering studies by one of Britain's most original and influential historians.

PADOVER, SAUL K. *The Revolutionary Emperor.* Rev. ed. Hamden, Conn.: Archon Books, 1967. An older but still useful work on Joseph II, one of the most interesting and complex of the enlightened monarchs.

PALMER, ROBERT R. *The Age of the Democratic Revolution: A Political History of Europe and America, 1760–1800.* 2 vols. Princeton, N.J.: Princeton University Press, 1959–1964. A major work of synthesis that views the revolutionary movements of the late eighteenth century as a transatlantic, rather than a mainly European or French, phenomenon. This work has aroused much controversy on both sides of the Atlantic. A good introduction to the debate is the pamphlet in *The Problems in European Civilization* series edited by Peter Amann, *The Eighteenth-Century Revolution: French or Western?* Boston: Heath, 1963.

RITTER, GERHARD. *Frederick the Great.* Trans. by P. Paret. Berkeley and Los Angeles: University of California Press, 1968. An historical profile of Prussia's great ruler by a leading German political and military historian.

ROSENBERG, HANS. *Bureaucracy, Aristocracy, and Autocracy: The Prussian Experience, 1660–1815.* Boston: Beacon, 1966. A superb study of the political and administrative centralization of Prussia.

SOREL, ALBERT. *Europe and the French Revolution: The Political Traditions of the Old Regime.* Trans. by A. Cobban and J. W. Hunt. Garden City, N.Y.: Doubleday Anchor, 1971. The first volume of *L'Europe et la Révolution française,* 9 vols. Paris, 1885–1911. A brilliant but cynical assessment of eighteenth-century diplomacy.

THOMSON, G. S. *Catherine the Great and the Expansion of Russia.* New York: Collier-Macmillan, 1962. A useful survey of another great empress, one of many women prominent in eighteenth-century politics and society.

TOCQUEVILLE, ALEXIS DE. *The Old Régime and the French Revolution.* Trans. by S. Gilbert. Garden City, N.Y.: Doubleday Anchor, 1955. A classic.

WILLIAMS, E. N. *The Ancien Régime in Europe: Government and Society in the Major States, 1648–1789.* New York: Harper & Row, 1970. A good recent state-by state survey that relates political developments to their social context.

SOCIETY AND ECONOMICS

The following works deal with the structure and material base of eighteenth-century European society.

ASHTON, THOMAS S. *An Economic History of England: The Eighteenth Century.* London: Oxford University Press, 1955. A substantial survey.

BARBER, ELINOR. *The Bourgeoisie in Eighteenth-Century France.* Princeton, N.J.: Princeton University Press, 1955. Despite its clumsy jargon, this is a penetrating socio-historical analysis of the class and its attitudes, values, and internal contradictions.

BEHRENS, C. B. A. *The Ancien Régime.* London: Thames and Hudson, 1967. Good introduction to French society of the period.

BRUFORD, WALTER H. *Germany in the Eighteenth Century: The Social Background of the Literary Revival.* Cambridge, Eng.: Cambridge University Press, 1956. First published in 1935, this is still the standard study in English.

CLIFFORD, JAMES L. (ed.). *Man versus Society in Eighteenth-Century Britain.* Cambridge, Eng.: Cambridge University Press, 1968. A collection of essays by distinguished scholars.

EINAUDI, MARIO. *The Physiocratic Doctrine of Judicial Control.* Cambridge, Mass.: Harvard University Press, 1938. An older but still outstanding study.

FORD, FRANKLIN L. *Robe and Sword: The Regrouping of the French Aristocracy after Louis XIV.* Cambridge, Mass.: Harvard University Press, 1953. A brilliant study of how the social reorganization of France came about and how it affected political thought and action and the power structure.

FORSTER, ROBERT AND ELBORG (eds.). *European Society in the Eighteenth Century*. New York: Harper & Row, 1969. Contains relevant documents and commentary on many social groups.

GOODWIN, ALBERT (ed.). *The European Nobility in the Eighteenth Century*. A collection of essays on the nobilities of all the major European countries. Those on England and France, by H. J. Habakkuk and J. McManners respectively, are especially good.

HECKSHER, ELI. *Mercantilism*. Trans. by M. Shapiro. Rev. ed. 2 vols. New York: Macmillan, 1955. A comprehensive survey of governmental economic policy throughout the early modern period.

HENDERSON, WILLIAM O. *Studies in the Economic Policy of Frederick the Great*. London: F. Cass, 1963. Studies by an authority on German economic history.

LANDES, DAVID S. *The Unbound Prometheus: Technological Change and Industrial Development in Western Europe from 1750 to the Present*. Cambridge, Eng.: Cambridge University Press, 1969. The first chapter of this definitive work examines the eighteenth-century background of the Industrial Revolution.

LOUGH, JOHN. *An Introduction to Eighteenth-Century France*. London: Longmans, Green, 1960. The best introduction in English to French society.

MCMANNERS, JOHN. *French Ecclesiastical Society under the Ancient Regime*. Manchester: Manchester University Press, 1960. Good analysis of the stablizing influence of the clergy.

MEEK, RONALD L. (ed.). *The Economics of Physiocracy*. Cambridge, Mass.: Harvard University Press, 1962. These essays examine the intellectual foundations of physiocracy.

SMALL, ALBION W. *The Cameralists*. Chicago: University of Chicago Press, 1909. An older but still useful study of the German and Austrian counterparts of the French physiocrats.

INTELLECTUAL AND CULTURAL LIFE

ADORNO, THEODOR W. AND MAX HORKHEIMER. *Dialectic of Enlightenment*. Trans. by J. Cumming. New York: Herder and Herder, 1972. A highly theoretical critique by two leaders of the Frankfurt school of social theory.

AUERBACH, ERICH. *Mimesis: The Representation of Reality in Western Literature.* Trans. by W. Trask. Garden City, N.Y.: Doubleday Anchor, 1957. Chaps. 16–17.

————. *Scenes from the Drama of European Literature.* Trans. by R. Manheim. New York: Meridian, 1959. Chaps. 3–6. Valuable essays by a distinguished German literary historian.

BABBITT, IRVING. *Rousseau and Romanticism.* New York: Meridian, 1957. First published in 1919, this essay is a provocative but distorted interpretation of Rousseau and his influence on modern thought by an American scholar who was influential during the early decades of this century.

BARTH, KARL. *Protestant Thought from Rousseau to Ritschl.* Trans. by B. Cozens. New York: Harper & Row, 1959. The first chapters of this work, by a leading Protestant theologian, are original and thoughtful.

BATE, WALTER J. *From Classic to Romantic: Premises of Taste in Eighteenth-Century England.* Cambridge, Mass.: Harvard University Press, 1946. Excellent essay on the transition from classicism to romanticism in English literature.

BECKER, CARL. *The Heavenly City of the Eighteenth-Century Philosophers.* New Haven: Yale University Press, 1932. A minor classic of interpretation discussed in the introduction to the present essay. Critiques of Becker's thesis are contained in Raymond O. Rockwood (ed.), *Carl Becker's Heavenly City Revisited.* Ithaca: Cornell University Press, 1958.

BERLIN, ISAIAH. *Vico and Herder: Two Studies in the History of Ideas.* New York: Vintage, 1976. One of the foremost philosopher-historians of the English-speaking world discusses two of the most important philosopher-historians of the eighteenth century.

BRIDENBAUGH, CARL. *Mitre and Sceptre: Transatlantic Faiths, Ideas, Personalities, and Politics, 1689–1775.* New York: Oxford University Press, 1962. Good study of the influence of the European Enlightenment on colonial America.

BRUFORD, WALTER H. *Culture and Society in Classical Weimar, 1775–1806.* Cambridge, Eng.: Cambridge University Press, 1962. Best work in English on the subject.

BRUNSCHWIG, HENRI. *Enlightenment and Romanticism in Eighteenth-Century Prussia.* Trans. by F. Jellinek. Chicago: University of Chicago Press, 1974. First published in 1947, this is an outstanding synthesis of social, political, and intellectual history by a distinguished French historian.

BURTT, EDWIN A. *The Metaphysical Foundations of Modern Science.* Garden City, N.Y.: Doubleday Anchor, 1955. A searching inquiry into the philosophical assumptions and implications of early modern science.

CASSIRER, ERNST. *The Philosophy of the Enlightenment.* Trans. by F. Koelln and J. Pettegrove. Boston: Beacon, 1964. First published in 1932, this is a brilliant work of intellectual history by one of Germany's foremost philosopher-historians.

———. *Rousseau, Kant, and Goethe.* Trans. by J. Gutmann, P. O. Kristeller, and J. H. Randall, Jr. Princeton, N.J.: Princeton University Press, 1945. The author, who long had a special interest in Rousseau, stresses here the continuity of his thought with that of Kant and Goethe.

COLLINGWOOD, ROBIN G. *The Idea of Nature.* New York: Oxford Galaxy, 1960.

———. *The Idea of History.* New York: Oxford Galaxy. 1956. The relevant chapters of both works, by the noted British idealist philosopher, are valuable.

CRAGG, GERALD R. *The Church and the Age of Reason, 1648–1789.* Harmondsworth: Penguin, 1960. Good survey of religion and the churches in general.

CROCKER, LESTER G. *An Age of Crisis: Man and World in Eighteenth-Century France.* Baltimore: Johns Hopkins University Press, 1959.

———. *Nature and Culture: Ethical Thought in the French Enlightenment.* Baltimore: Johns Hopkins University Press, 1963. Both works are close examinations of the intellectual and moral theories and problems posed by the Enlightenment.

DARNTON, ROBERT. *Mesmerism and the End of the Enlightenment.* Cambridge, Mass.: Harvard University Press, 1968. Good study of the radical temper of the generation which preceded and initiated the revolution.

DURKHEIM, ÉMILE. *Montesquieu and Rousseau: Forerunners of Sociology.* Ann Arbor: University of Michigan Press, 1965. An early work by one of the pioneers of modern sociology.

ECHEVERRIA, DURAND. *Mirage in the West: A History of the French Image of American Society to 1815.* Princeton, N.J.: Princeton University Press, 1957. A carefully documented case history of

French public opinion between 1767 and 1815.

FOUCAULT, MICHEL. *Madness and Civilization: A History of Insanity in the Age of Reason*. Trans. by R. Howard. New York: Pantheon Books, 1965. A fascinating study of attitudes toward insanity in the early modern period by a leading contemporary French thinker.

GAY, PETER. *The Party of Humanity: Essays in the French Enlightenment*. New York: Norton, 1971.

––––––. *Voltaire's Politics: The Poet as Realist*. New York: Vintage, 1956.

––––––. *The Enlightenment: An Interpretation*. 2 vols. New York: Vintage, 1966–1969. Three major works by one of the most distinguished American scholars of the Enlightenment.

GREEN, FREDERICK C. *French Novelists, Manners, and Ideas: From the Renaissance to the Revolution*. New York: Ungar, 1964. Good survey by a long-time authority on French literature.

HALL, ALFRED R. *The Scientific Revolution, 1500–1800*. Rev. ed. Boston: Beacon, 1966. Authoritative but fairly technical.

HARRIS, RONALD W. *Reason and Nature in the Eighteenth Century, 1714–1780*. New York: Barnes and Noble, 1969. Good general work on English thought and culture.

HAUSER, ARNOLD. *The Social History of Art*, vol. III: *Rococo, Classicism, Romanticism*. Trans. by S. Godman. New York: Vintage, 1958. Rich in erudition and insights.

HAVENS, GEORGE R. *The Age of Ideas*. New York: Holt, Rinehart & Winston, 1955. Deals with the development of the Enlightenment through an examination of the careers of leading *philosophes*.

HAZARD, PAUL. *The European Mind, 1680–1715*. Trans. by J. L. May. Cleveland: Meridian, 1963.

––––––. *European Thought in the Eighteenth Century: From Montesquieu to Lessing*. Trans. by J. L. May. Cleveland: Meridian, 1963. Two comprehensive reconstructions of intellectual history.

HIGHET, GILBERT. *The Classical Tradition: Greek and Roman Influences on Western Literature*. New York: Oxford Galaxy, 1957. Chaps. 18-19. Good discussion of the classical elements of the Enlightenment.

KANN, ROBERT A. *A Study in Austrian Intellectual History: From Late Baroque to Romanticism*. New York: Praeger, 1960. One of the few works in English in this area by an authority on Habsburg history.

KEDOURIE, ELIE. *Nationalism*. New York: Praeger, 1961. The early chapters reconstruct the eighteenth-century philosophical foundations of later nationalism.

KELLY, GEORGE A. *Idealism, Politics and History: Sources of Hegelian Thought*. Cambridge, Eng.: Cambridge University Press, 1969. An excellent study of the development of idealist philosophy from Rousseau to Hegel.

KOYRÉ, ALEXANDRE. *From the Closed World to the Infinite Universe*. New York. Harper Torchbook, 1958. A brilliant philosophical critique of the development of early modern science.

KRAUS, MICHAEL. *The Atlantic Civilization: Eighteenth-Century Origins*. Ithaca: Cornell University Press, 1966. First published in 1949, this is a good study of the intellectual and cultural relations between Europe and America.

LEVEY, MICHAEL. *Rococo to Revolution: Major Trends in Eighteenth-Century Painting*. London: Thames and Hudson, 1966. An excellent work of art history and interpretation.

LOVEJOY, ARTHUR O. *The Great Chain of Being*. Cambridge, Mass.: Harvard University Press, 1936.

———. *Essays in the History of Ideas*. Baltimore: Johns Hopkins University Press, 1948. Important essays on the origin and development of various aspects of eighteenth-century thought by one of America's most distinguished intellectual historians.

LUKÁCS, GEORG. *Goethe and His Age*. Trans. by R. Anchor. An important collection of essays on German literature of the period, written during the 1930s and 1940s, by a leading Marxist theorist and literary historian.

MANUEL, FRANK E. *The Prophets of Paris*. New York: Harper Torchbook, 1965.

———. *The Eighteenth Century Confronts the Gods*. New York: Atheneum, 1967. Two important works of interpretation by one of the most distinguished American historians of the Enlightenment.

MARTIN, KINGSLEY. *French Liberal Thought in the Eighteenth Century: A Study of Political Ideas from Bayle to Condorcet*. New York: Harper Torchbook, 1963. First published in 1929, this is still the best introduction to the political thought of the French Enlightenment.

MAY, HENRY F. *The Enlightenment in America*. New York: Oxford University Press, 1976. A good recent synoptic study of the Enlightenment in America.

NEFF, EMERY. *The Poetry of History: The Contribution of Literature and Literary Scholarship to the Writing of History since Voltaire*. New York: Columbia University Press, 1947. Part one examines eighteenth-century historical thought.

PALMER, ROBERT R. *Catholics and Unbelievers in Eighteenth-Century France*. Princeton, N.J.: Princeton University Press, 1939. Good reconstruction of the conflict between French Catholic thinkers and the free-thinking *philosophes*.

PAYNE, HARRY G. *The Philosophes and the People*. New Haven: Yale University Press, 1976. A fresh look at the attitudes of the *philosophes* towards the lower classes.

REILL, PETER H. *The German Enlightenment and the Rise of Historicism*. Berkeley: University of California Press, 1975. The only comprehensive study of eighteenth-century German historical thought in English.

ROBBINS, CAROLINE. *The Eighteenth-Century Commonwealthman*. Cambridge, Mass.: Harvard University Press, 1959. A good study of the relationship between intellectual, political, and social history.

STEPHEN, LESLIE. *English Thought in the Eighteenth Century*. 2 vols. New York: Harcourt, Brace & World, 1962.

———. *English Literature and Society in the Eighteenth Century*. London: Methuen, 1963. Although published in the first decade of this century, both works are still useful and informative.

VENTURI, FRANCO. *Utopia and Reform in the Enlightenment*. Cambridge, Eng.: Cambridge University Press, 1971. A detailed study of the republican tradition in the development of the Enlightenment by a distinguished Italian historian.

VEREKER, CHARLES. *Eighteenth-Century Optimism*. Liverpool: Liverpool University Press, 1967.

VYVERBERG, HENRY. *Historical Pessimism in the French Enlightenment*. Cambridge, Mass.: Harvard University Press, 1958. Two contrasting interpretations of the Enlightenment conception of the past and future.

WADE, IRA O. *The Clandestine Organization and Diffusion of Philosophic Ideas in France from 1700 to 1750*. Princeton, N.J.:

Princeton University Press, 1967. A good reconstruction of an important aspect of the Enlightenment.

WASSERMAN, EARL R. (ed.). *Aspects of the Eighteenth Century.* Baltimore: Johns Hopkins University Press, 1965. A collection of essays on various aspects of eighteenth-century thought and culture by distinguished scholars.

WATT, IAN. *The Rise of the Novel.* London: Chatto & Windus, 1957. A good study of the eighteenth-century English novel.

WILLEY, BASIL. *The Eighteenth Century Background.* Boston: Beacon, 1961. A good introduction to English thought of the period.

WOLF, ABRAHAM. *A History of Science, Technology, and Philosophy in the Eighteenth Century.* Rev. ed. New York: Harper Torchbook, 1961. Packed with information, but poorly conceived and organized.

A few of the works in foreign languages, which were especially helpful in the preparation of this essay, should be mentioned here.

ANTONI, CARLO. *Der Kampf wider die Vernunft: zur Entstehungsgeschichte des deutschen Freiheitsgedankens.* Trans. from Italian by W. Goetz. Stuttgart: Koehler, 1951. A penetrating inquiry into the idea of freedom in eighteenth-century German thought by a distinguished Italian intellectual historian sympathetic to Croce's philosophy.

EHRARD, JEAN. *L'idée de Nature en France a l'Aube des Lumières.* Paris: Flammarion, 1970. An excellent study of the Enlightenment conceptions of nature and scientific method and their application to man and society.

KRAUSS, W. AND H. MEYER (eds.). *Grundpositionen der französischen Aufklärung.* Berlin: Rütten & Loening, 1955. A collection of essays on various aspects of the French Enlightenment by noted East German scholars. Although written from an orthodox Marxist viewpoint, they are scholarly and offer a challenging alternative to the liberal viewpoint to which English readers are usually exposed. Also contains an extensive bibliography with a special section on Soviet scholarship. See also Krauss's *Studien zur deutschen und französischen Aufklärung.* Berlin: Rütten & Loening, 1963.

MAUZI, ROBERT. *L'idée du Bonheur dans la Littérature et la Pensée française au XVIII siècle*. Paris: Colin, 1960. A major work of interpretation packed with penetrating insights into the ideological implications of eighteenth-century French thought and literature.

WORKS ON INDIVIDUAL THINKERS

The following are but a few of many useful studies of major figures of the Enlightenment.

ALLISON, HENRY S. *Lessing and the Enlightenment*. Ann Arbor: University of Michigan, 1966.

BARNARD, FREDERICK M. *Herder's Social and National Thought*. Oxford: Clarendon Press, 1965.

COBBAN, ALFRED. *Edmund Burke and the Revolt against the Eighteenth Century*. 2nd ed. New York: Barnes and Noble, 1960.

CROCKER, LESTER G. *Diderot: The Embattled Philosopher*. New York: Free Press, 1966.

GRAY, RONALD. *Goethe: A Critical Introduction*. Cambridge, Eng.: Cambridge University Press, 1967.

GRIMSLEY, RONALD. *Jean D'Alembert, 1717–1783*. Oxford: Clarendon Press, 1963.

JORDAN, DAVID P. *Gibbon and His Roman Empire*. Urbana: University of Illinois Press, 1971.

KETTLER, DAVID. *The Social and Political Thought of Adam Ferguson*. Columbus, Ohio: Ohio University Press, 1965.

KNIGHT, ISABEL. *The Geometric Spirit: The Abbé de Condillac and the French Enlightenment*. New Haven: Yale University Press, 1968.

MACK, MARY P. *Jeremy Bentham: An Odyssey of Ideas*. London: Heinemann, 1962.

REGIN, DERIC. *Freedom and Dignity: The Historical and Philosophical Thought of Schiller*. The Hague: Martinus Nijhoff, 1965.

SHACKLETON, ROBERT. *Montesquieu: A Critical Biography*. London: Oxford University Press, 1961.

SHKLAR, JUDITH. *Men and Citizens: A Study of Rousseau's Social Theory*. London: Cambridge University Press, 1969.

SMITH, DAVID W. *Helvétius: A Study in Persecution*. Oxford: Clarendon Press, 1965.

STEWART, JOHN B. *The Moral and Political Philosophy of David Hume*. New York: Columbia University Press, 1963.

WADE, IRA O. *The Intellectual Development of Voltaire*. Princeton, N.J.: Princeton University Press, 1969.

WILSON, ARTHUR M. *Diderot: The Testing Years, 1713–1759*. New York: Oxford University Press, 1957.

ANTHOLOGIES

Most of the major writings of the leading enlighteners are readily available in satisfactory English editions. Below is a selection of useful anthologies.

BERLIN, ISAIAH (ed.). *The Age of Enlightenment*. New York: Mentor, 1956.

BRINTON, CRANE (ed.). *The Portable Age of Reason Reader*. New York: Viking, 1956.

CAPALDI, NICHOLAS (ed.). *The Enlightenment*. New York: G. P. Putnam, 1967.

GAY, PETER (ed.). *The Enlightenment*. New York: Simon & Schuster, 1973.

TORREY, NORMAN L. (ed.). *Les Philosophes*. New York: Capricorn, 1960.

INDEX